CREATING
CEREMONIES

Innovative Ways to
Meet Adoption Challenges

Cheryl A. Lieberman, Ph.D.,
and
Rhea K. Bufferd, LICSW

Zeig, Tucker & Co., Inc.
Publishers
Phoenix, Arizona

Library of Congress Cataloging-in-Publication Data

Lieberman, Cheryl A.
    Creating ceremonies : innovative ways to meet adoption challenges
/ Cheryl A. Lieberman and Rhea K. Bufferd.
        p.   cm.
    Includes bibliographical references.
    ISBN 1-891944-10-X
    1. Adoption rites.   I. Bufferd, Rhea K.   II. Title.
GT2460.L54   1998
394.2—dc21   98-30945
                                                                        CIP

Pubished by

ZEIG, TUCKER & CO., INC.
1928 East Highland, Suite F104-607
Phoenix, Arizona 85020

Manufactured in the United States of America

10   9   8   7   6   5   4   3   2

In memory of my mother, Ilaine, and my sister, Bonnie, for believing
in my abilities and allowing me to experience the strength of
good mothering and the close friendship possibilities of siblings.

In honor of my father, S. Bernard (Buddy), for his unconditional support
and for showing me that loving parenting never ends.

In honor of my sons, Eric and Christopher, for helping to enhance
my creativity and resourcefulness and for challenging me
to be a better person.

—Cheri Lieberman

To my husband, Allan, whose love and confidence in me have
enriched my life.

To my children, Lauren and Steven, who have provided me with
the true rewards of parenthood.

—Rhea Bufferd

Table of Contents

Acknowledgments

THE AUTHORS WISH to thank the following for their input and assistance at various stages in the process of putting an idea into words and transforming those words into a book: The Stars of David, Carolyn Smith and the Massachusetts Adoption Resource Exchange, Denise K. Maguire and Sandra Foti of Cambridge Family and Children's Services, and Joan L. Clark and the Open Door Society. Also, Joyce Wesson, Bruce Sunstein, Dan Soyer, Carol B. Sheingold, Jane Saks, Corinne Rayburn, Joyce Maguire Pavao, Debra N. Olshever, Edie Arnowitz Mueller, Edward Miller, Sheila McIntosh, S. Bernard Lieberman, Susan Landers, Sharon Kaplan-Roszia, Faith Hamlin, Melissa Fay Greene, Linda Gold-Pitegoff, Mimi Doe, Allan S. Bufferd, Juliet Askenasae, and Rev. Fred W. Anderson.

Cheri Lieberman wishes to express special thanks to others who offered encouragement: Nancy Zare, Joshua Weiss, Mary Urban, Cynthia Siegel, Lynn Sanford, Mary Rusk, Ellen Rockefeller, Ellin Reieisner, Joan Rachlin, Janet McGovern, Fred Miller, Rus Lyman, Susan and Joseph Kolb, Lissa Kapust, Betsy Jacobs, Robert and Susan Hill, Roberta Hershon, Diane Halperin, Heather Hall, Susan Gotshalk, Lynda Girard, Edwin Davidson, Adina Davidson, Helen Cohen, Chrissy Carew, Khouri Jamison Carlen, Kim Breas, George Berry, Ann Abrams—and Nancy Weiss was always there with suggestions, advice, and a listening ear.

Rhea Bufferd would like to acknowledge, in particular, support from Elie and

Alan Persky, Ann Mitchell Ivy Bufferd, Marilyn Wilcher, Merle and Sarah Westlake, Jane Sullivan, Roberta Pressman, Harriet and Sam Miller, Leigh Gray, Cal Fuller, and Jennifer Benson.

Finally, the authors acknowledge the efforts of Bernie and Ella Mazel, as well as Suzi Tucker and Jeffrey K. Zeig of Zeig, Tucker & Co. in bringing our project to fruition.

Foreword

Sharon Kaplan Roszia, M.S.

R ITUALS OFFER THE possibility of healing, clarifying, and bridging, as well as the gift of continuity in our lives from birth to old age. Some rituals are planned and are seen as real benchmarks in life's journeys; others are almost unconscious as they form the everyday patterns of life. Think for a moment about the annual rituals of birthdays, anniversaries, and the holidays by which we mark the seasons of the year. Examine the weekly and daily habits of our lives that become unconscious for us.

I remember the Friday night dinners at my maternal grandmother's home with all my aunts, uncles, and cousins: real chicken soup for the soul along with matzo balls, homemade oatmeal cookies, and peanut butter cookies with the "crisscross" sign on the top. These were gatherings of connection, security, and warmth that shaped my childhood into my teenage years.

When nervous at night, especially during big Midwest thunderstorms, my sister and I would comfort each other by shining our flashlights on the ceiling and creating animal shadows or "dancing" together with our lights. Many years later, as adults, we were comforting each other through a tough time when my sister handed me a flashlight so that I could "dance" with her on the ceiling.

Rituals are powerful containers of emotion that we can draw upon as we wish for comfort, clarity, and memory. The world of adoption has not traditionally tapped into this rich resource. Only in the past few years, have we begun to use rituals in workshops at adoption conferences to address and redress the pains and gains of those touched by this powerful institution. I have had the privilege of joining with other workshop presenters in leading as many as 175 adoptees, birth parents, adoptive parents, and social workers through ceremonies that have transformed attendees' emotional experiences.

A practitioner of open adoptions for the past 20 years, I know of no better way of clarifying the parties' roles and boundaries in these expanded clans. Entrustment, entitlement, and naming ceremonies are a regular part of open adoptions. Marriages of clans for the sake of children so that they don't have to lose relatives to gain relatives, as well as in-family, kinship adoptions where grandparents become parents and parents become aunts and uncles-all require rituals to cement these new relationships.

The missing elements of applying the gifts of ceremony are addressed in this wonderful book. Cheryl Lieberman and Rhea Bufferd have combined their professional training and their knowledge of children and adoption so that parents and therapists can bring the powerful healing elements of rituals to children and their families. I am convinced, both as an adoptive parent and as a social worker, that these techniques are absolutely necessary in helping children sort out the past, clarify the present, and become open to the attachments offered in new families. Rituals speak to both the verbal and preverbal aspects of the child. Children who may be stuck, afraid, or confused can move forward in their new homes if some of these powerful, but simple, strategies are employed. I pray that families will find their way to this book and uncover both their own and their children's creativity and joy by participating in the ceremonies offered here.

Preface

THE AUTHORS, Cheri and Rhea, began their working relationship long before
the ideas for this book were conceived. It started in 1986 when Cheri went
to the agency where Rhea worked to discuss her desire, as a single mother, to
adopt an older child.

Cheri had attended adoption information sessions at several agencies, so that
when she arrived at the Cambridge Family and Children's Service, she said that
she felt welcomed and accepted. She met with Rhea for an initial consultation
there, and Rhea both listened to her needs and respected her concerns.

According to Rhea, she can still remember how impressed she was by how
thoroughly Cheri had thought through her decision to adopt, studied her options,
and had her supports in place—including her parents, her sister, and members
of her extended family. She made sure that Rhea had a chance to meet and talk
with all of them.

Cheri said that the home-study process was exciting, helpful, and enlightening.
Rhea took Cheri through a series of issues and asked her to think about whether
she could picture herself as a parent under various circumstances. For example,
could Cheri imagine herself as a parent to a child who was retarded? What about
a child whose parents were alcoholics or were addicted to drugs? What if the child
grew up to have problems with substance abuse? Every question Rhea asked

challenged Cheri's values, strengths, and limitations. For Cheri, the home study clarified the issues that she might have to face, issues that she had not thought about before.

Rhea's agency approved Cheri's home study and she was matched with a seven-year-old boy whose biological brother lived in a foster home where adoption was the goal. Both boys had had difficult early-life experiences and would require patience and commitment from their adoptive families, as well as a willingness for them to maintain their relationship. (Two years later, when the younger brother's placement could not move ahead to adoption, it was natural for the two to be reunited in Cheri's home.)

Cheri had visited with her son in his foster home to get to know him before he moved into her home. She created her first ceremony as a way to overcome their anxieties on the day he arrived. It worked!

Rhea continued to work with Cheri after the placement and realized the helpfulness of her use of ceremonies as problems arose. Rhea had begun her work in adoption in 1968, a time when the number of available infants was decreasing owing to the legalization of abortion and the diminishing stigma of "out of wedlock" births. Prospective families were being asked to consider children two years of age and older. These children had been placed in the care of the State because their birth parents had proved unable to care for them, and they often lived in several foster homes before a permanent placement was found. Such children presented a challenge to adoptive parents. It was a case of "love is not enough," and the families needed resources to assist them. The needs were there before the knowledge about how to help was readily available and social workers experienced frustration when asked to provide the families with the skills they would need to make the placements work. And those who worked with families adopting older children were virtually learning on the job.

Rhea also realized that the feelings of helplessness that older children engendered in their new parents made their lives difficult, and if the situation continued long enough, that often signaled the beginning of the end of the placement. Creating a ceremony was a way for such parents to engage in a concrete activity that would provide a structure in which both the parent and the child could address the problem at hand.

Over time, we came to believe that ceremonies could help many adoptive families, and the social workers involved with them, and were looking for a way to share this technique. The result was this book.

As others became aware that we were working on the book, we were invited to give workshops on the subject of ceremonies for adoptive parents and professionals working in the field of adoption. We believe strongly in the benefits of adoption and are grateful for the opportunity to provide whatever assistance we can in making it more viable for families and children.

Rhea Bufferd and Cheri Lieberman

∝ 1 ℘

Getting Started

WHY CEREMONIES?

CHILDREN COME INTO families through various ways—birth, adoption, divorce, remarriage. In the main, the child-rearing issues facing most families are similar, including safety, discipline, responsibility, independence. But for families that adopt a child, such matters as identity, self-esteem, loss, and transitions take on unique meanings and added complexity.

The outstanding characteristic of adoption lies in how it provides a way to fulfill the needs of everyone involved. The birth parents can be sure that their child will be raised in a family with love and security; the adoptive parents have the opportunity to nurture and raise a child they might otherwise have not had; and a child can grow in a stable, loving home. But even with all these happy assurances, there is an undercurrent of sadness. Each of the parties to an adoption has experienced a profound loss that will affect his or her life for years to come. Birth parents who decide to relinquish their child because of problems in their own lives, or who have been forced to give up their parental rights by court order, have lost a child. Whether it is an infant who has shared the birth mother's body and thoughts for nine months or an older child who has been an ongoing or intermittent part of his or her parents' lives for a number of years, the loss is significant for both the parents and the child. Adoptive parents also suffer a loss—that of not actually giving birth to the child and of not having a child who replicates themselves. For both the biological and adoptive parents, the intense feeling of loss may be mitigated by time, but for the child, the reverse may be true, as a growing awareness of what it means to be adopted raises questions about his or her genetic past and future.

This undercurrent of loss, with its accompanying feelings of sadness, is usually not articulated, and may even be denied. Biological parents are encouraged to forget and to go on with their lives. Adoptive parents are focused on the joy of finally having a child on whom to lavish their love and attention. They may experience disappointment or concern about the quality of their attachment to their adopted child, or of the child's to them, but having waited so long and worked so hard to each this goal, they may not want to give voice to these feelings. And the adopted child may not understand or have the words to express the complicated feelings stirring inside. Instead, the child may act out this inner turmoil in behavior that creates problems for the family.

Fortunately, help for families dealing with adoption issues is becoming more accessible. In recent years, adoption has changed from a secretive, shameful choice to one that is more open and accepted, although the advantages and the losses are still open to discussion. No longer is an adopted child's wish to learn about his or her biological beginnings and to meet one day with the birth parents seen as a negative reflection of his or her adoptive parenting. As society has condoned the search for one's ethnic and racial roots, so too has there been an ever-growing acceptance of an adopted person's right to know.

The problems inherent in raising a child not one's own by birth have been deemed a natural consequence of adoption and are being studied in an effort to find solutions. Research studies have resulted in new techniques for evaluating families, such as ecomaps and genograms, and new methods to deal with behavior problems are being developed. The number of books written about all aspects of adoption has increased dramatically. A monthly newsletter, *Adopted Child*, and a magazine, *Adoptive Families*, provide valuable resources for these families. This attention to adoption has helped all parties involved to feel more normal, and more able to share their concerns and seek help.

A technique that we have found helpful is the use of rites, rituals, and ceremonies. Although such activities in general are common in family life, rites specific to the adoption situation are almost nonexistent. Several recent books have recognized the value of ceremonies in our lives. *Rituals for Our Time* by Evan Imber-Black and Janine Roberts (1993), both family therapists, shows the powerful role that rituals play in the family and their use in therapy. Randolph Severson (1991), of the Hope Cottage Adoption Center in Dallas, in *Adoption: Charms and Rituals for Healing* uses poetry and stories to illuminate the special issues adoptive families face. Mary Martin Mason's (1995) *Designing Rituals of Adoption for the Religious and Secular Community* helps families develop ceremonies to mark the important events related specifically to adoption.

The present book focuses on how the use of ceremonies can provide a short-term solution to problems facing adoptive families that can threaten their stability and well-being. We have found that ceremonies written specifically to address a difficult issue that has arisen can help the child to overcome the experience of loss and disappointment. These ceremonies can also help to alleviate the feelings of futility that overwhelm adoptive parents as they contend with their child's difficult behavior or fears. They afford a way for parents and children to bond. The ceremonies can be enhanced by eating special foods, lighting candles, showing physical affection, or even giving a small token or gift. Children of all ages thrive on routine and repetition, the familiar and the expected. Once performed, these ceremonies can be repeated as often as the child likes.

The following chapters present actual scripts of a broad range of rituals and ceremonies to assist adopted children, their parents, and the professionals who support them. Specific ceremonies are described that can help children to deal with the various issues that confront them and their families as they adjust to a life together—transitions, self-esteem, loss, fears, learning, remembering. The ceremonies discussed here are designed for such real-life situations as how to prepare an adopted child for a second adopted child or a birth child's coming into the family; how to help the child ignore all the bad messages he or she received; or how to help a child believe that even though he or she was abandoned by his birth parents, his adoptive parents will stick with him. The book teaches you how to create your own ceremonies for situations specific to your child. We have chosen not to designate age ranges for those participating in a ceremony because of the children's varying language and comprehension abilities, especially those whose early life experiences were traumatic. Generally, the ceremonies, as written, are for children with some reading ability—ages 7 to 14. Most can be modified for children in the three- to six-year range, and some can be adapted for 15- to 17-year-olds. Most chapters include additional suggestions for ceremonies specifically designed for nonverbal children and for those for whom English is a second language.

We have tried to make the book broad in scope so that the ceremonies cover both the preadoptive phase, when the child and family are just getting to know each other, and the actual moving in and continuing adjustment problems. There are ceremonies, as well, to mark events throughout an adopted child's childhood and adolescence.

We have included all kinds of families—two-parent, single-parent, biological-parent, foster-parent, and adoptive-parent families, as well as families with gay and lesbian parents and those of multiracial, multiethnic, or multicultural origin. We address what occurs as the result of the ceremonies, what to do if something goes awry, and how to handle a negative outcome.

We know how hard most adoptive parents try to help their children. We have learned much from the adoptive families who attended our workshops, and have incorporated their suggestions into this book. Our goal has been to enhance what adoptive parents are already doing to improve their family lives. We want to expand their repertoire. We are aware, however, that ceremonies do not make permanent changes in a child's personality or behavior; rather, they are short-term solutions to help families get through crises so they can continue to stay together.

We begin with a ceremony that can give structure and certainty to an anxiety-producing moment—when you finally bring an adopted child home to live with your family.

THE "COMING HOME" CEREMONY

The new mother goes to the foster home to pick up her new child. There is a mingled look of happiness and nervousness on the boy's face as he greets her at the door. She puts the two large, green garbage bags containing his possessions into the trunk of the car, and waits while he says his farewell. Together they get into the car and leave.

On the way home, the mother tells the boy how excited she is that he is with her, and she confesses a little nervousness, too. Mostly, she tells him she is glad to be taking him home. Then she tells him that as soon as they first walk into the house, they will do a special ceremony to welcome him home. In the car, the mood shifts from anxiety to anticipation.

It is early Saturday afternoon and the sun is shining brightly. The new mother and son walk into the house together, carrying his two green garbage bags. Putting the bags down, they both walk into the living room, where two large cushions have been placed side-by-side on the hardwood floor. Each cushion has a sheet of paper lying on it. The mother and then the child each picks up a sheet of paper and sits on a cushion. She helps him light two candles that are on the floor next to the pillows. The "Coming Home" ceremony begins.

"COMING HOME"

ERIC:
My name is Eric. I am seven years old and today I am moving into my forever home with my forever family. Pepper will be my forever cat. Cheri's parents will be my forever grandma and grandpa. Cheri will be my mommy* forever. She will take care of me, feed me, play with me, and help me when I am sick. She will hug me and cuddle me and give me attention. Even if I feel angry or say I want to leave and live with someone else, this will always be my home and Cheri will always be my mommy. I will try to listen to her. Even if I do not listen to her sometimes, she will still be my mommy. I will try to do good things. Even if I do bad things, this will still be my home forever and Cheri will still be my forever mommy.

CHERI:
My name is Cheri. Today is the day that Eric moves in to stay and I become his forever family. Pepper will be his forever cat. My parents will be his forever grandpa and grandma and I will be his mommy forever. Wherever I live will be Eric's home too. Even when he grows up and wants to have his own place to live, this will always be his home. I will take care of him, feed him, play with him, and help him when he is sick. I will buy him clothes and toys, cuddle him, hug him, and give him attention. Even if Eric feels angry or says that he wants to leave and live with someone else, this will always be his home and I will always be his mommy. Eric will try to listen, and even if he does

---

*If your child has difficulty saying "mommy" or "daddy," you can substitute the word "parent." Some children may feel disloyal to their biological or foster parent(s) and some may distrust the permanency of this new relationship. Still others may use "mommy" and "daddy" generically without emotional attachment.

not listen to me sometimes, I will still be his
mommy. Eric will try to do good things, and even if
he does bad things sometimes, this will still be his
home forever, I will be his forever mommy, and he
will be my forever son.

During the month of preadoptive visiting, the child had been to the house and
asked if certain rooms and furniture would be his when he moved in. So after
they read their parts (the mother helped her son with the big words), the child
blew out the candles and the mother started to walk him through the house
saying, "This is now *your* living room." Her son quickly corrected her and said,
"This is *our* living room." And so it went as they walked through the house—
stairs, kitchen, bathroom, and so on. Their life together had begun.

HOW TO USE THIS BOOK

Please use this book in the way that works best for you. You do not have to
read it from beginning to end to find it useful. You can adapt the ceremonies to
reflect the issues on which your family would like to work.

"Why Bother" with creating a ceremony? The "why" is discussed from both a
parent's perspective and a professional's perspective. Each view is based on experience and the way each sees the situation from the vantage point of the roles
they play.

Sometimes a ceremony works, and sometimes it doesn't. "How to Create a
Ceremony" shares what the authors have learned. Simple guidelines and related
rationales are there, as well as what to do if your child can't read and/or is nonverbal.

The sample ceremonies are categorized by themes for easier focus, and each
category includes some thoughts on their relevance to adoption. The ceremonies,
of course, may fit more than one circumstance. While you may want to customize
them for your own family, you are welcome to use the examples as they are.

The sample families reflect the variety of family types in the adoption community today. If your type of family type was omitted, please let the authors know
so that they can learn, too. If yours is one of the many families with a rich cultural,
ethnic, religious, or other heritage, let your family's ceremonies reflect that
uniqueness.

Some of the best moments can come in the context of "spontaneous ceremonies" and "magic ceremonies." Children have the gift of imagination. If we follow their lead, they can make things happen that create special memories.

Under "Special Situations," you will find some thoughts to consider if you adopt an infant, a teenager, or a child from a different race or culture.

The "Barriers" section highlights some reasons why ceremonies may not work for you. Read this part especially if you find yourself saying, "Yes . . . but . . ."

Most of all, the authors hope that this book will allow you to explore additional resources to support your family, and to have fun in the process.

WHY BOTHER?

A PROFESSIONAL VIEW

Rituals and ceremonies mark the milestones in our lives. They provide us with the opportunity to celebrate, to remember, to hope, and to mourn. We observe birthdays with parties where we blow out candles marking the years of our lives; we celebrate weddings and anniversaries by envisioning the future or remembering the years we have been with our spouses; and we mark the ending of a life with rituals rooted in our culture and religion.

Because adoption is a different way of becoming a parent, many of the rituals in which biological parents participate are missing from adoptive parenthood. When a woman is pregnant, her friends and family help her to prepare for the birth by "showering" her with gifts for the new baby. When the baby is born, the father hands out cigars and the parents send birth announcements. Religious ceremonies, such as baptism, christening, circumcision, and naming, celebrate the new addition to the family.

Several factors make these rituals more difficult for adopting parents. They do not know how long they will have to wait for a placement, and they do not know exactly how old the child will be. The child may still be legally bound to one or both biological parents, and there is a waiting period mandated by the State before the adoption can be legalized. These factors contribute to the insecurities the new parents may be feeling and make them reluctant to plan such events as christenings and baptisms. Whereas biological families take these rituals for granted, adoptive parents often cannot.

It is best that adopting parents also observe these traditional rituals. Showers given for you by family or friends when you adopt a child can make you feel more "normal." But if adoptive parents are uncomfortable with public ceremonies before the legal issues are resolved, they can create their own ceremonies to welcome the child into their home. When the child's adoption has been legalized, the family can participate in the religious and traditional rituals with extended family and friends.

Ceremonies created for specific situations can be helpful for both adoptive parents and their children. They provide a way for them to feel close and to build a basis for their future life together. They also offer an opportunity to share the range of feelings, from joy to sadness, that come with adoption. There is such excitement at the coming together of parents who truly want a child and a child in need of a loving family that it's not surprising that the sadness and loss that are also a part of adoption are ignored.

Many adoptive parents come to adoption because of problems of infertility. They have suffered the loss of not creating a child out of their love for each other. In their pain, they may also have come to identify with the loss felt by the birth parents of the child they are adopting. The child has also suffered a loss, that of his or her birth family. He or she will not understand or may not have the words to express the complicated feelings stirring inside. Rather, these feelings may go underground and surface in behaviors ranging from withdrawal, depression, and aggressiveness to perfect, "don't rock the boat," and anxious to please. Such behaviors can be difficult for adoptive parents to understand. Whether they have adopted an infant or an older child, they are anxious to be good parents and to give the child what he or she needs to grow into a happy, responsible adult, and will be bewildered and overwhelmed by a backlash of negative behavior. Their feelings of confusion can be damaging to the parent–child relationship, and can lead to withdrawal or inappropriate discipline, which may polarize the relationship even more. Ceremonies can help adoptive parents understand and cope with their feelings of helplessness in the face of a child's difficult behavior, and can help the child, as well, by focusing on these concerns.

Many older children waiting to be adopted have led chaotic lives without the comfort of normal everyday routines, which contributes to their fears and insecurities. A ceremony written specifically for a child dealing with a difficult issue can provide a predictable format to replace previous experiences with instability. Ceremonies and rituals truly create a way for parents and the child to bond.

The one ceremony that is unique to adoption is legalization, which takes place in the judge's chambers in court after a period of time designated by the State. The judge has received the official papers from the agency overseeing the adoption and signs the adoption decree in the presence of the adoptive family and their guests. This process is apt to be perfunctory and brief, but adopting families can enhance the day by inviting grandparents and very close friends and family members to the legalization. Many families continue the celebration by going out for brunch or giving a party at home. Pictures taken at the courthouse and with the judge are a wonderful reminder of this special occasion. They may then celebrate the anniversary of this special legalization day in the years that follow and establish individual rituals to mark the importance of the day in their lives.

A PARENT'S VIEW

Cheri started to do ceremonies on the day Eric came to live with her. They had been visiting for one month and she realized that the first moments at home would be awkward for both. During the month of visiting, Eric had shared his confusions and fears, directly and indirectly. Conversation was hard for him. He had been in several placements that had not worked out and so had no reason to believe that Cheri was really going to be his mother. In fact, when he said that he would be with Cheri forever, he defined it as "until his next birthday." He had tested her during the month of visiting—throwing tantrums in stores and being generally defiant. He had had enough false starts that this probably felt like a make-or-break situation. How do you convey to a child who has been let down by adults that you keep commitments and that he is here to stay? He had heard this message from adults before.

The fact that a child is older when adopted means that the adoptive family misses out on many of the ceremonies and rituals that would, or should, have taken place early in the child's life. Cheri thought that a "Coming Home" ceremony would help start a family ritual and say the words that he needed to hear. Eric responded so well to the ceremony that Cheri felt that she had found a method of connecting that could be useful. In fact, every time that Cheri and Eric went out that week (it was during a school vacation) and came back into the house, he wanted to do the ceremony (minus "the tour"). When Cheri adopted Christopher, Eric's biological brother, two years later, she also used ceremonies with him.

Ceremonies can be used to get through tough moments, as well as for celebrations. They are not the answer to everything for every family, of course, but a ceremony can provide you with a sense of helping to give perspective to the present and create the future.

Both Eric and Christopher were adopted when they were over six years old. And as is true of most children who are adopted when they are older, they had been legally removed from their birth family because they had suffered serious and prolonged abuse and neglect. Their birth parents evidently had done the best they could, but had very limited parenting skills. This lack of good parenting resulted in many challenges for the children, which surfaced almost as daily occurrences.

We need to help each other learn new ways of meeting such challenges. In this book, Cheri, as an adoptive mother, has combined ceremonies she did with and for her own sons with those she created for others. The names of the others involved are fictitious, but the ceremonies themselves and the issues they address are true to actual experiences.

HOW TO CREATE A CEREMONY

THE PURPOSE

Every ceremony needs a reason that makes sense to both the children and parents. Remember, though, that they are meant only to focus on immediate issues; long-term problems cannot be solved overnight. They are not a cure, but an opportunity to reframe the present. What works for one transition may not work for another. So while the language may be similar, no two ceremonies are ever the same. They depend on the specifics of the circumstances and the child's language ability and vocabulary. Among the topics of the ceremonies described here are transitions, self-esteem, loss, learning, fear, remembering, anger, and as celebrations of anniversaries and other events.

WHAT WORKS AND WHAT DOESN'T

The actual text of the ceremonies is not hard to write. Cheri is aware of this because she hates to write and has been known to freeze over a writing assignment. It took her almost six years of prodding to attempt this book. Think of a ceremony as like a conversation with a child—how you envision it might go if everyone was saying what they wanted and needed to say.

Although you do not need major writing skills, you do need an awareness of what is going on with your child. When the child acts in ways that say, "Send me away," is he or she really asking for reassurance that you will love him or her no matter what? If the child's social worker is moving to a new job, how can your child be helped to say goodbye to this social worker and hello to the new one?

You may make mistakes. When a ceremony is created for the adults and not for the children, they may say the words, but in a disconnected way. When adult words or concepts are used instead of those of the children, they became distracted. When there are too many words or the ceremony is too long, the children lose interest. When the issues involved are too sophisticated, the words die on the paper.

When the ceremony relies on the children's own words, it feels real to them. When they have a lot of short things to say, they stay interested. When children have activities to do as part of the ceremony, the message is reinforced. When the ceremony addresses a current, relevant issue for the children, they feel really heard. When it has one theme only, the repetition of that theme helps the children to remember the message.

You will notice very few contractions (such as "can't" and "don't") in the text for these ceremonies. The reason is that many children have trouble reading contractions at a young age, although they can say them. Also, it is made clear that participants can change their parts if what they are to say does not feel right for them.

Repetition is important for children. Research has indicated that ideas must be repeated at least four times to be absorbed. Moreover, most children love repetition. They can read books and watch videos over and over again. Children will respond enthusiastically to repeating the same lines within ceremonies, or even similar ideas from one ceremony to another. Some of the most repetitive ceremonies, where each person in the ceremony reinforces the same thoughts, are often the children's favorites.

You may, of course, use the ceremonies presented in this book as written, but those that you create out of your own experience will have more meaning for you. If you are nervous about doing that, consider adapting the ceremonies in the book to your situation, using language that might be closer to what you and your child would say.

As you plan ceremonies, keep in mind that the child's reading and verbal abilities are important considerations. If your child is a strong reader, give him or her more to read. That also keeps his or her attention more focused on the ceremony.

Most of the ceremonies in this book do not include roles for the biological parents. If you have an open adoption, and the biological parents are able and willing to take part, you are encouraged to include them if it makes sense for the situation and the child and you are comfortable. It should not be done because it is a "nice" thing to do, but because it will enhance the life of the child. At no time should anything be embarrassing or uncomfortable. It will come through no matter how well you think it can be covered up. Ceremonies are for healing, not for hurting. They are for reframing, not for creating issues. Sharon Kaplan-Roszia and Lois Melina (1993), in the book *The Open Adoption Experience*, refer to an entrustment ceremony at which biological parents entrust the adoptive parents with the child. If the circumstances are right, the biological family can be included in a variety of ceremonies, such as the "Name-Giving" ceremony.

You might start to do a ceremony and find that it is not working. It is okay to acknowledge that, and to do it either at another time or in another way. Let the others, including your child, help to make it work. If you are clear about your purpose, just follow the principle of equifinality from systems theory: you have a clear target and recognize that there may be hundreds of ways to achieve it. If you are stuck because your purpose or message is muddled, get clear and try again. If you have a child who might focus on your mistake, see that as an opportunity to demonstrate that you are not perfect.

WHAT IF YOUR CHILD IS NONVERBAL OR CAN'T READ?

If your child is nonverbal or can't read, you are faced with some extra challenges. Do not let that throw you. You have learned to communicate with your child in other ways—just incorporate them into this process. You might use more pictures, either having your child draw how he or she feels or point to a picture of a face that represents his or her feelings. Some very special moments in life do not require words.

This is also a good time to use your child's game-playing skills. A family therapy technique that uses the idea of the old game of "Statues" is called "Family Sculpture." You ask your child to create a scene using real people in the family, pillows, stuffed animals, or toys to represent different things, and then try to put words around what he or she did. If the child is unable to use words, you can then interpret what you see. Then check with the child to be sure you are interpreting things correctly. In fact, all of those who participate can comment on how they feel about their position in the scene or about the scene itself. Everybody willing to do so might take turns directing the arrangement, which would give their perspective as well. Most children enjoy the opportunity to tell adults what to do.

In a game played with infants, a parent asks, "How much do I love you?" and then stretches the baby's arms out as far as they will go and says, "This much," which represents a major universe for the baby. Or the parent asks the same questions and stretches his or her own arms out as far as they will go.

Another idea is to use simple puppets with different expressions on their faces. You can tell stories and ask the children to use whatever puppet fits what they are feeling and have the puppet do whatever they are feeling. In this way, you can put words to what they are trying to convey. It helps to learn from one another.

In a ceremony centering around saying goodbye to a home, the parent could say words of farewell and have the child wave goodbye to all parts of the home without saying a word. One could also envision a child's saying "hello" to a new home with a hello gesture to all the new spaces. If you think of mime as a way of expressing real ideas, nonverbal possibilities seem endless. A child could do a goodbye or hello dance of his or her own creation—no music necessary. You could also bake something in the old home and eat it in the new one.

Perhaps a young boy with attention-deficit/hyperactivity disorder (ADHD) is coming to live with you. You might take pictures of different rooms in the house and give them to him on the day before he moves. If he visited earlier, he could try to remember which rooms these are or you could tell him. You might show him a picture of what will be his room and tell him that when he arrives, you want to take a picture of him sitting in his room to make this picture complete. Then when he arrives, have him walk though the house with you, matching the pictures to the rooms and take an instant photo of him so he can see that now all is complete.

During a conference session on rituals and ceremonies, some participants came up with an idea for a ceremony in which you would take a large ribbon and to it tie other ribbons, each representing a home a child has lived in before coming to yours. It creates a sense of history without a lot of words. Other participants suggested that if there are two teenagers, one new to the family, you could take them into the woods and have them gather pieces of wood for a fire that would be large enough to require two people to carry the wood—thus their having to work together.

One professional shared that she had a special place in her office where she keeps items that people can use to create ceremonies together by starting with a purpose for the ceremony and then selecting objects to be tools in the ceremony they create together. You are only as constrained as your imagination.

When doing ceremonies around remembering, parents could say what they remember and ask the child to nod his or her head or blink an eye if the child remembers too. If children are fearful when a parent leaves on a trip, that parent could develop a ritual to be done each time he or she leaves to reassure the child and another ritual to confirm that the parent is coming back.

In one case of a woman with a biological infant, each morning just before leaving the house she hugs the baby, says she loves her and will see her later, and then rubs noses with the baby. One day she came back in the house because she forgot something. The child cried because the regular ceremony had been disrupted by her return. The woman tries not to forget things, but when she does, she repeats the ceremony so that her child feels reassured.

Even a bedtime routine becomes a comforting ceremony that speaks to stability in our children's lives. Many of the children who are adopted after infancy have not experienced much permanency on which they could rely. A simple nighttime routine can offer that. Most of us do daily ceremonies and rituals with our children

that we do not think about. Just extend that ability to planning one-time ceremonies or allowing spontaneous ceremonies to evolve.

You and your children will discover together what works best and is most
effective. There is no right way, but there is always a good way. If you have a
partner or a spouse, you may find you have different ways of approaching ceremonies. Experiment and look for what works for your family. And have fun.

WHEN IS THE BEST TIME?

Don't have a ceremony, even if you have planned to do it on a particular night:

- If any participant is overtired or irritable (this includes you).
- If it is too close to bedtime (sometimes feelings get stirred up that need
processing time).
- If something has happened that would make the ceremony not relevant at
that time.
- If you and your child are angry with each other, resolve the anger first, the
ceremony won't do it.
- If homework is unfinished, since concentration after a meaningful
ceremony may be jeopardized, even for good reasons.

Check with your child to see if he or she is up for a ceremony. If the child is
not, postpone it, unless doing so would defeat the purpose. For example, in the
"Saying Goodbye to Our Old Home" ceremony, holding off until the day after
you have moved makes no sense. Giving a token item to children enhances their
interest, especially around difficult topics. For example, one might give a small
figure of a lion and say, "I'm not 'li-on' when I say I love you," or a tiny bear and
say, "I love you 'beary' much." It does not even have to be creative, but it's better
not to give money—it feels too much like a bribe.

An important note: Do not do a ceremony just before you leave the house for
the evening or go on a vacation. Children may need some time for talking, questions, or a hug.

WHO PARTICIPATES IN A CEREMONY?

Who participates in a ceremony? That depends on who is around and who is
appropriate. With the "Name Giving" ceremony, for example, you could include
whoever happens to be there, and give each person at least one line to say. At
this ceremony, the child can receive his or her new last name even before it is
legally changed. This adds to the sense of belonging. If a ceremony is definitely

for the child and the parent alone, no one else should participate, even if they are there. They can listen from another room or watch if that feels okay. When Cheri and her sons did "This Is Me, This Is Us" about being part of the family and still being able to pull away and be themselves, she chose not to include her mother's helper; even though she is an integral part of their lives, she is not an official member of the family.

WHERE DOES IT TAKE PLACE?

Where in the house or apartment a ceremony is conducted depends a lot on the type of ceremony and the dwelling. For example, you might sit on big cushions in a central place in the living room. It is preferable that the floors be uncarpeted because you can then safely light candles to mark the start of a ceremony and blow them out to mark its close. Otherwise, you can either put the candles on a metal tray or use medium-sized decorative candles that come in glass candle holders, such as votive candles. Lighting candles as part of a ceremony makes the moment official and special, and grabs kids' attention. Keep in mind, though, that some circumstances and ceremonies do not lend themselves to lighting candles—especially if children are having problems with matches and fire in general. Sprinkling some potpourri in a bowl of water can be just as effective.

Make the space as distraction-free as possible—no radios or TVs, one telephone not in the same room off the hook (preferable to answering machines, which still have telephones ringing); and no music. While some might feel that music in the background lends to the occasion, it also can divert a child's attention.

Also, "where" does not have to be the same place every time. If you or your child wants to experiment with different spaces, do so. The best place for a fish funeral, for example, is the bathroom: "From water he came, to water he shall return."

❧ 2 ❧

Ceremonies of Celebration

> *"Name Giving"*
> *"Forever Family"*
> *"Honoring the Child"*

A MONG THE JOYS of life for both adults and children are celebrations of birth-days, anniversaries, weddings, confirmations, bar and bat mitzvahs, and first communions. These events honor the celebrants and underscore the importance of these occasions in their lives. As rites of passage, they offer an opportunity to reflect on the past and to plan for the future. Along with celebrations of cultural, ethnic, and religious holidays, they connect us to the past as the rituals are passed down from generation to generation.

Even if children who are adopted after years of living with birth and foster families have celebrated some of these occasions, it is unlikely that there has been much continuity. The new adopting family can provide this by incorporating the child into its traditions. Acknowledging the importance of the child's past by including any traditions he or she may have enjoyed with other families can be very validating for the child. If a child is adopted from another country, the new family might want to learn about how events are celebrated there and incorporate these traditions into its own celebrations.

Adoptive families will want to add to the occasions that they usually celebrate to acknowledge the specialness that adopting has brought to them. The "Name Giving" ceremony celebrates the first step in the child's becoming a part of your family. The "Forever Family" ceremony marks the day of legalization when the child officially becomes a family member. "Honoring the Child" is a special ceremony to confirm extended-family relationships as the child is welcomed into the larger family circle.

~

SITUATION
Giving a child your last name before legalization.

A social worker had suggested that Elizabeth give her last name to 7½-year-old Kamir soon after he moved in. Elizabeth's mother had flown in from Ohio to help her and a cousin had joined them for dinner. The ceremony was another way of telling Kamir that he really was a part of this family, that he belonged. Some children and adoptive parents may choose to retain the child's original last name as a middle name. Changing a child's name is not the only way to help him or her belong.

"NAME GIVING"

COUSIN BUDDY:	When I became a son, my parents gave me their last name.
GRANDMA:	When Elizabeth became my daughter, Grandpa and I gave her our last name.
MAMA:	Now that you are my forever son, I will give you my last name. With this "Name Giving" ceremony, I give you my last name to be your last name, too. That tells people that we are a forever family. I am your forever mommy and you are my forever son. Your name is now Kamir Anderson.
KAMIR:	Because we are a forever family, you are giving me your last name to be my last name. My name is now Kamir Anderson. Buddy is my forever cousin. Grandma and Grandpa are my forever grandparents. Elizabeth is my forever mommy and I am her forever son. My name used to be Kamir Singh, and that was a good name. My new name, Kamir Anderson, is a good name, too. With this "Name Giving" ceremony, my name is now Kamir Anderson.
Group hug	

AFTERWARDS

Kamir was thrilled with his new last name. Teachers had been alerted to use his new name and reported to Elizabeth that he seemed very pleased.

~

SITUATION

Giving a child who cannot read your last name before legalization.

Three years after Elizabeth had adopted her first son, she adopted a second, Kamen, who was Kamir's biological brother. She wanted to do another "Name Giving" ceremony, but her new son could not yet read. Also, Kamir had mixed feelings about the new addition to the family. Elizabeth decided that Kamir could act as the big brother that he was and feel a little more in control if he helped Kamen to say his part. The "Name Giving" ceremony was further complicated by the fact that the last foster family had hoped to adopt Kamen, and even though they never legally changed his last name, they would tell him he was a Fentner. So Kamen came with the confusion of two last names. Cousin Buddy and his parents were with them that evening.

"NAME GIVING"

MAMA:	When I became a daughter, Grandma and Grandpa gave me their last name.
AUNT IRMA:	When I became a daughter, my parents gave me their last name.
UNCLE HENRY:	When I became a son, my parents gave me their last name.
COUSIN BUDDY:	When I became a son, Uncle Henry and Aunt Irma gave me their last name.
KAMIR:	My name used to be Kamir Singh, and that was a good name. Now that I am part of a forever family, I was given the name Kamir Anderson, and that is a good name, too.
MAMA:	Kamen, now that you are my forever son, I will give you my last name. With this "Name Giving" ceremony, I give you my last name to be your name, too. That tells people we are a forever fam-

ily. I will be your mother forever and you will be my son forever. Your name is now Kamen Anderson.

KAMIR HELPS KAMEN READ:

Kamen, repeat after me:

Because we are a forever family
I have just been given
the name Anderson
to be my last name.
Elizabeth is my forever mommy
and you are my forever brother.
We will live together in the same home.
I used to have the name Singh or Fentner.
Those are good names.
My new name is Kamen Anderson.
That is a good name, too.

KAMIR: Yes, with this "Name Giving" ceremony, your new name is Kamen Anderson. Welcome to our family name.

MAMA: And welcome, again, to our family.

KAMEN SHAKES EVERYONE'S HANDS.

Group hug

AFTERWARDS

Kamen spent the rest of the evening practicing his new name—saying it and printing it with Kamir's help. Elizabeth had alerted his teachers and others involved, so that they would start using Kamen's new name. This affirming process seemed to make Kamen "sparkle" the next day. Belonging is a different issue than legalization.

SITUATION
After a disappointing legalization event.

Manuel, a single father, went to court to have the adoption of his seven-year-old son, Carlos, finalized. The court formality proved disappointing. Manuel tried to help the moment by having pictures taken. He had also given Carlos an ID bracelet with Carlos' new initials and the date to help mark the occasion. In spite of his efforts, he left feeling that it was a letdown. Manuel's father, who had flown in for the official day, shared Manuel's sentiments. Manuel decided to set up a ceremony. Most children probably understand the concept of "blood brother." When speaking of their families, people often refer to them by saying, "blood of my blood and flesh of my flesh." So, he thought, why not incorporate that concept into the ceremony? In this day of AIDS, mixing blood with another can make some people nervous. If you do not want to touch fingers, each person can put some blood on a plate and you can use an implement to mix the drops of blood. This is definitely a ceremony in which only actual family members should participate. An alternative would be to take a lock of hair from each person and make a nest.

"FOREVER FAMILY"

PAPA:	While we have been a family in our hearts, today we become a forever family officially. I think that today is the best day I have ever had.
GRANDPA:	While you have been my grandson in my heart for a long time, today we have become granddad and grandson officially. Today, I feel very lucky.
CARLOS:	When I first came here, we had a "Coming Home" ceremony. Papa and I talked about how we were a forever family. I liked the ceremony but I was not sure I really believed it. Today, I really believe it and I know it is true.
PAPA:	I want to say again my promise to you. I promise to • provide you with love and family • help you grow in body, mind, and spirit • respect your memories of your life before you came to live with me • help keep ongoing connections to your birth mother and father and your brothers and sisters
CARLOS:	I want to say again my promise to you. I promise to • accept your love • accept your help in guiding me to do my best • accept your helping me grow to be healthy in body, mind, and spirit

Blood-mixing ceremony or nesting ritual
EACH PERSON SAYS HOW HE OR SHE FEELS.

EVERYONE: Our forever family ceremony is over. No one can
                      ever separate us. This is for keeps.

Group hug

AFTERWARDS

*This ceremony was much more satisfying than the actual moment in court,
which felt more intimidating to Carlos than exciting. The home ceremony felt
more official, too. It was helpful to the father and grandfather, as well, in
underscoring the importance of the occasion.*

⌒

SITUATION

Grandparents want to enhance their attachment to their grandchild.

*Sally and Lisa, a lesbian couple, had adopted nine-year-old Marsha. Sally's
mother decided that she and her husband would like to do a ceremony honoring
the child when she visited them during a school break.*

"HONORING MARSHA"

This ceremony is to honor Marsha Petrosky (a reconfigured last name) as the
forever daughter of Sally Petran and Lisa Triosky and the forever granddaughter
of Susan and Chet Triosky.

MARSHA: My name is Marsha Petrosky and today marks the
                      three-month anniversary of my legally being Marsha
                      Petrosky. Sally and Lisa will be my mothers forever,
                      and when I am home with them in Virginia, they
                      will take care of me, feed me, and help me when I
                      am sick. They will hug me and cuddle me and give
                      me attention. Wherever Sally and Lisa live, I will
                      live, and they will be my forever mothers.

NANA: My name is Susan Triosky and I am Sally's forever
                      mother and Marsha's forever grandmother. I live in

	Michigan. I love Marsha and I love Sally, and whenever Marsha is with me I will take care of her and feed her and hug her. I will try to help her learn new things. Even if Marsha feels angry, I will always love her. When Marsha feels sad, I will try to help her feel happy.
GRANDPA:	My name is Chet Triosky. I am Sally's forever father and Marsha's forever grandfather. I live in Michigan. When Sally was a little girl, I took care of her, and played with her, and gave her lots of hugs. Whenever Marsha is with me, I will take care of her, and hug her, and play with her. Even when Marsha feels angry, I will love her. I know Marsha tries to listen to me, and even if she does not listen to me sometimes, I will be her forever grandfather. I will always love her.
MARSHA:	When I was adopted, I became your legal granddaughter, and we all became relatives. Sally and Lisa are my mothers forever, and Nana and Grandpa are my forever grandparents. I will try to listen and I will try to do good things. I know that Nana and Grandpa love me, and I love them.
COMMENTS:	(Anyone):
EVERYONE:	We are glad we are relatives.
Hugs all around	

AFTERWARDS

Using a method that Marsha felt was a family experience helped to underscore the message of family. The grandmother wrote the ceremony, which helped her to connect. The ceremony broke through the awkwardness of beginning. It also helped the grandparents to attach to Marsha and it helped her to clarify and confirm the relationships. They all enjoyed it. They said it was a wonderful ceremony.

NONVERBAL ALTERNATIVES: CELEBRATIONS

Children love to make chains out of colored construction paper and paste. Each family member could be assigned his or her own color. While sitting together around a table or on the floor, each member could make loops that represent himself or herself. Strips of paper could be precut. After everyone made a decided-on number of loops (cuts down on the competition), the loops could be put together in various orders to show that everyone was now connected to everyone else. The resulting chain could be hung as a symbol of family togetherness. It would symbolize that everyone is part of the family and everyone represents an important link in the chain and family. This might be a good way to demonstrate that whether a child is in a family through birth or by adoption, all are connected, important, and unique.

The blood mixing, as in blood brothers/sisters, could also be used alone as a nonverbal alternative (see the "Forever Family" ceremony) so that children can see part of themselves mixed with parts of other family members. For health and safety reasons, different, sterile needles are used to prick the finger of each person and an implement is used to mix the blood on a plate or in a bowl.

❧ 3 ❧

Ceremonies for Transitions

"Going, Coming, and Staying"

"Getting Ready for a New Person in the Family"

"Welcome Home"

"Returning Home"

"End of the School Year"

"I Entrust You with My Child"

"A New Addition Is Coming/Has Arrived"

TRANSITIONS ARE ESPECIALLY difficult for adopted children. Often they have been moved from one family to another with minimal or no preparation. Even with the best-thought-out explanation, the child may be too traumatized by the move to understand what is being said. He or she is left feeling insecure and unsure as to whether or when the next move will come.

As adopted children get older, they may experience all transitions with uncertainty and fearfulness. Starting school, going to summer camp, visiting grandparents in another town, hospitalization—events such as these may heighten the fear of the unknown. A ceremony designed to express sadness for what is being left behind and hope for what the next step will bring can be comforting for the child. It allows for the unspoken, and often unrecognized, feelings to be named, accepted as normal, and put into perspective. Many ceremonies created to deal with loss can also be used for transitions, as each move forward implies the loss of what is left behind.

The "Going, Coming, and Staying" ceremony speaks to the normality of transitions in all lives. It goes on to the specific changes with which each child has had to deal and names the feelings engendered by the change. It offers hope for new relationships.

The "Getting Ready for a New Person in the Family" ceremony helps to prepare a child for a new sibling. It speaks of the negative feelings a child may have, as well as the positive ones. Composing the "Welcome Home" ceremony for the new sibling can be a family effort, with a major role played by the child already in the family.

The "Returning Home" ceremony welcomes a child who has been away and can be used for difficult separations, such as hospitalizations, as well as for vacations.

The "End of the School Year" ceremony gives the child the opportunity to reflect on the past year's experience and to prepare for the next one.

The "I Entrust You with My Child" ceremony represents a transition for all the adults present, as well as for the baby. It gives the birth mother and the new adoptive parents the opportunity to openly express the range of feelings they are experiencing. Although the baby is too young to understand the emotional components, his or her well-being is enhanced by this process that supports the adults.

The "A New Addition Is Coming to Our Family" and "A New Addition Has Arrived" ceremonies help the other children in the family to prepare for, and then welcome, a new baby. It is used to teach the children about adoption and the mixed feelings they will have, and to reassure them of their parents' love for them.

⌒

SITUATION
A child becomes upset whenever someone leaves.

Nancy and Vernon had adopted 13-year-old Shirley three years earlier. Although they have provided a stable home, every time someone leaves, even temporarily, Shirley falls apart. The parents wanted to help Shirley try to grasp the concept that some people go and some come, some stay and some don't. Shirley needed to learn that just because people are out of your sight, unless they have died, you can still stay in touch. It is like the very young infant who thinks that if something is not in sight, it has disappeared. One of the joys of peek-a-boo is the fact that the person reappears. The truth is that with most adopted children, people who disappear from their lives do not try to keep in touch. Also, children have less control over staying in touch than do adults. Nancy also wanted to reassure Shirley that she was staying, and that the fact that a sitter left did not mean that anything was wrong with Shirley. Nancy and Vernon had done some ceremonies with Shirley, so the concept was not foreign to them.

"GOING, COMING, AND STAYING"

DAD:	Life is a series of people coming and going—some stay and some don't.
SHIRLEY:	It can be hard when people you care about go and do not come back right away.
MOM:	Yes. I have found that the more you let yourself get close to people, the more their leaving hurts. But if you never allowed yourself to get close in the first place, you would never have experienced the joy.
SHIRLEY:	I hate it when people go away, even for a short time. I feel angry, upset, scared, left behind, and lonely.
DAD:	The hardest going away is when someone dies because you will never see the person again. When my sister died, I was very sad that I would never see her again. I was mad at her for dying but I was also glad that she had been a part of my life.
SHIRLEY:	Most of the people who have gone away from me are not dead, so I can see them again, write to them, or talk with them on the phone. I may feel mad that they left, but I can feel happy that they were, and are, a part of my life.
MOM:	Ms. Fitzgerald came into your life and ours. She has been a good teacher and friend. She needs to go to get her heart fixed so she is going away for a while. I look forward to the time we can see her again.
SHIRLEY:	Phyllis came into my life and yours. She has been a good therapist and friend. Now she needs to stop working so she can have her baby and stay home with her two children. I am mad that she is leaving, but I am happy that she has helped me so much and been my friend. I will probably see Phyllis again, not as my therapist, but as my friend.
MOM:	And other people have come into your life.
SHIRLEY:	That is true. A new mother who loves me very much; Alicia, Kevin, Max, and other family members who love me bunches. And then there is

	Lewis. When I look at the "coming" side, it is pretty full.
DAD:	Yes, remember when your favorite sitter, Brian, left and we thought we would not see him for a very long time? Look what happened.
SHIRLEY:	Yes, Brian came back.
MOM:	So we need to let ourselves feel all our feelings, the good ones and the bad ones, the happy ones and the sad ones, the confusing ones and the clear ones.
SHIRLEY:	And we need to look around and see that people come and go in our lives, and to remember that some people stay.
DAD:	Yes, no matter what.
SHIRLEY:	You both stay.
MOM AND DAD:	Yes.
SHIRLEY:	Grandma stays.
MOM:	Yes.
SHIRLEY:	And Grandpa stays.
DAD:	Yes.
SHIRLEY:	Alicia, Kevin, and Max stay.
MOM:	Yes.
SHIRLEY:	And I stay.
MOM AND DAD:	Yes, this is your home always and you are in our hearts always. Even when you grow up and want to live in your own place, you will stay in our hearts always. We love you very much.

Hug time

AFTERWARDS

The ceremony kept Shirley's attention in a way that previous attempts at discussion had not. She stayed very alert throughout. She read her part with a lot of inflection. The words seemed to mean a great deal to her. The actual impact was hard to assess.

⌒

SITUATION
Getting a first child ready for a second child's coming into the family.

Tom and Andy, a gay couple, adopted Jinwei, who is 12, four years earlier. Jinwei has thrived in a household where he is the only child. He was entering a critical time developmentally, and his parents were concerned about how to introduce the fact that another child would be coming into the home. They decided to let him be part of the second-child decision. When they talked to Jinwei, at times he seemed to be happy, and at other times, not very enthusiastic about the prospect. Tom and Andy thought that a ceremony might help set the stage for seven-year-old Daniel to come into the home and have a special moment with Jinwei.

"GETTING READY FOR DANIEL"

POP:	Someone you might live with With the same last name too. It's not your dad or cat. It's someone true blue.
DAD:	Sometimes they're a pest And sometimes they're a bother. They are better known as
JINWEI:	A sister or a brother. Some of the nice things about having a brother are: • It makes things more interesting. • It makes things more fun sometimes.
POP:	• You are not so lonely. • Sometimes they help.
JINWEI:	• I have someone to play with.
DAD:	Sometimes, you might not like having a brother because: • You have to share Pop's and my attention with him and you want us to yourself all the time.
JINWEI:	• He may borrow stuff and not take care of it. • He may tease me, pick on me, fight with me, tell on me, and embarrass me.

Pop:	We can help turn some of these into rules to help you and Daniel get along. For example, one rule could be: Take care of the things you borrow. Maybe you can think of others and the four of us can talk them over.
Jinwei:	Daniel and I can help each other by listening and trying to understand each other's feelings.
Dad:	That's true. And you and Daniel are unique and special in your own ways. We love you because of who you are and we hope that we will love Daniel the same way.
Pop:	We will love both of you differently, in a special way for each of you.
Jinwei:	I am worried that you will love Daniel better or more.
Dad:	At moments, we may like better what one of you is doing. Even if we do not like what you do, that does not mean that our loving for you gets smaller. It gets bigger over time. Do you believe that?
Jinwei:	(Answers Yes or No and says why.)*
Pop:	So next week we welcome Daniel into our family forever with open arms and open hearts. And re-member, you are already here.
Hugs	

AFTERWARDS

Previously, when Tom and Andy had tried to discuss Daniel's coming to the home with Jinwei, they found him unresponsive. They opted to use the ceremonial technique to try to get certain messages across to Jinwei in a timely fashion. They found him more open to talking with Daniel in the days after the ceremony.

Special note to parents: If the child answers "No," be sure to offer reassurances that loving gets bigger over time.

⌒‿

SITUATION
Welcoming a second child into a home.

Andy and Tom and their adopted son, 12-year-old Jinwei, for the last five weeks have been visiting with Daniel, a seven-year-old boy who is coming to live with them and to be adopted after the waiting period. The week before, Andy and Tom did a ceremony with Jinwei to help him get ready to welcome Daniel into their home and family. Jinwei agreed that a ceremony to welcome Daniel into the home when he arrived would be good. They asked him if he wanted to help create it, and he said No, but he would like to participate.

"WELCOME HOME, DANIEL"	

ANDY:	My name is Andy. Today is the day that Daniel moves in to stay.
JINWEI:	This place will be Daniel's home forever—the same way it is mine.
TOM:	My parents will be your grandmother and grandfather forever. I will be Jinwei's and Daniel's father forever.
JINWEI:	In this house, you will be safe. Tom and Andy will take care of you, feed you, play with you, and help you when you are sick. They will hug you and cuddle you and give you attention.
	Daniel, please say this after me:
	Even if I feel angry
	Or say I want to leave and live with someone else
	Tom and Andy will always be my fathers.
	I will try to listen to them.
	Even if I do not listen to them sometimes, they will still be my fathers.
	I will try to do good things.
	Even if I do bad things, this will still be my home forever and Andy and Tom will still be my forever fathers.
ANDY:	Yes, all of that is true. Jinwei knows that we keep

	our promises. Daniel, you will learn that in time, too.
TOM:	We know that today can feel many different ways— happy, sad, scary, excited, confusing, and more. All of those feelings are all right. We feel some of them, too. We will help each other with all the feelings that anyone has. Deal?
JINWEI AND DANIEL:	Deal! (Shake hands.)
JINWEI:	We all have a lot to learn about being a family. We will make some mistakes, but we will try to do our best. Daniel, I promise to help you, and will you promise to help me?
DANIEL:	(Yes or No)
TOM:	And we will help, too, and we will learn from both of you, as well.
ANDY:	We have love for two, so welcome, Daniel, and know that you are home—Jinwei, Daniel, Tom, and me.
TOM:	We are a family forever.
Family hug	

AFTERWARDS

Tom and Andy wanted to use a technique that had worked well for Jinwei to welcome Daniel into the home even though they did not know how well Daniel could read, and so had to take this into account when developing the ceremony. They decided to have Jinwei help Daniel, to make him feel important. Daniel loved being helped by Jinwei, and he also loved the ceremony. It was a positive moment to say some things without being preachy.

⌒

SITUATION

A child who was hospitalized following a suicide attempt is returning home and has asked for a ceremony to welcome her back.

Lydia is a single mother with two adopted daughters, Celine, who is 14, and Adina, who is 12. The adoptions were open ones, which allowed Celine to see her birth mother twice a year and Adina to see her birth mother three times a year. When Celine's birth mother relocated to another state, the twice-yearly visits stopped. Although other types of communication were still possible, the move brought back feelings of being left behind for Celine. She was overwhelmed by them, and tried to hang herself. Lydia acted quickly and Celine was admitted to a psychiatric setting for three weeks. When Celine was about to come home, she told Lydia that she needed a ceremony to welcome her back. Lydia developed this ceremony in less than 10 minutes, after they arrived home. Among the welcoming group were the grandfather and Lydia's household helper, Corinne.

"RETURNING HOME"

MOM:	At different times, each of us may leave home for short periods of time. This time, Celine left.
CELINE:	Yes, I needed some special help and left home to get it.
CORINNE:	I was glad you were able to get the help you needed.
GRANDDAD:	So was I.
ADINA:	So was I.
MOM:	Now we are all here and celebrating being together as a family.
CELINE:	Sometimes being together as a family is hard and sometimes it is easy.
ADINA:	Sometimes being together as a family is hard and sometimes it is easy.
GRANDDAD:	Being home with your family means that you can be all of who you are. You do not have to pretend to be someone or some way you are not. And a family loves you just the way you are.
CORINNE:	In a family, people love you because you are a part of that family.
CELINE:	In this family, I am loved because of who I am.
ADINA:	In this family, I am loved because of who I am.
MOM:	I sometimes think I am the luckiest mother in the world to have two such special daughters.
GRANDDAD:	And I think to myself sometimes how lucky I am to have two such wonderful granddaughters.
CORINNE:	And I think sometimes how lucky I am to be working with two such terrific girls.

CELINE:	Even when I was away, I was here in people's minds and hearts. This is my family forever.
ADINA:	And I missed you. I like playing with you and I am glad you are home.
GRANDDAD:	And I am glad you are home.
CORINNE:	And I am glad you are home.
MOM:	And I am glad you are home.

Group hug

AFTERWARDS

Celine had experienced ceremonies before and had felt their benefit. She loved her ceremony. She needed reassurance that she was okay and still welcome in the family. Asking for a ceremony to welcome her home was easier than clearly saying what she needed. A ceremony does not have to be long or involved to meet its objective. What may seem like a lot of repetition to an adult is useful to a child.

SITUATION
Two sons express sadness about the end of the school term.

Peter is a single father with two adopted sons—Sylvan is 11 and Mark is nine. Usually both boys cheer when school is over, but this year was different. They had been talking a lot at the dinner table about how much they were going to miss their teachers and their classmates over the summer. Both boys would be moving from contained classrooms to regular classes, and that held some fear as well. Therefore, the conversations were unusually charged. Peter thought it might be helpful to put their thoughts and feelings into perspective while honoring their sadness. He developed a ceremony to do all of these things.

"END OF THE SCHOOL YEAR"

SYLVAN:	Today was the last day of school for this year for me.
MARK:	Today was the last day of school for this year for me, too.

SYLVAN:	Ending the school year means that I will not see some people I like as often.
MARK:	Ending the school year means that I will not see teachers I like during the summer.
DADDY:	It also means thinking about all that you have learned this year. Why not say some things you have learned this year?
SYLVAN:	(Says what he learned.)
MARK:	(Says what he learned.)
DADDY:	And what do you think you will miss the most?
SYLVAN:	(Says what he will miss the most.)
MARK:	(Says what he will miss the most.)
DADDY:	What do you think you will miss the least?
SYLVAN:	(Says what he will miss the least.)
MARK:	(Says what he will miss the least.)
DADDY:	This day also marks two new beginnings.
MARK AND SYLVAN:	It marks the start of camp next week. We are going to Camp Ledoli. It marks the beginning of the new school year to come. This school year will be very special for both of us. We will both be going into regular classes. We are going into regular classes because we are smart and can learn.
MARK:	It may be hard for us because it will feel so different.
SYLVAN:	It may be hard for us because the demands will be greater.
DADDY:	Yes, and I will be here to help you be successful. And so will all your teachers. Most of all, you will be helping yourself.
SYLVAN:	We will try our best.
MARK:	We will try our best.
DADDY:	That is all anyone can do. We can also do some things to get you more ready. Over the summer, we can continue to read together and practice writing and math—just a little—not too much.
SYLVAN:	We can do a little practicing, like athletes do.
MARK:	Yes, we can practice like basketball players do, only we will practice what we need for school.

Daddy:	Maybe we will practice using games and contests so it will be fun.
Mark:	We can have fun at camp and fun at home and fun doing some practicing.
Sylvan:	We can talk more about games and contests and come up with ideas we like.
Daddy:	Mostly the summer is for playing, with a little bit of practice slipped in.
Sylvan:	So here is to our new beginning.
Mark:	To our new beginning.
All:	Yay, group!
Group hug	

AFTERWARDS

The ceremony was well received and seemed to help both boys adjust to the change. They were in better spirits the day after the ceremony and were focused on going to camp.

⌒

SITUATION

Birth parent passes the care of her baby to a preadoptive couple.

Jeannie, who was 19 and wanted to go to college, had given birth to a healthy baby girl six months earlier. She realized that she could not be a parent to her daughter and put her life together simultaneously. She genuinely wanted the best for her daughter, and a social worker connected her to Arnie and Ruth, who wanted a child and had been waiting for three years to adopt one. The three adults met and decided to proceed with an open adoption. After all the legal steps were taken, they held an entrustment ceremony that had been written by the three together with the social worker. The social worker agreed to videotape the ceremony, which took place at the agency, so that the infant would have it as part of her new beginning. Both families would receive copies of the videotape. At the ceremony, Jeannie held her daughter, who was asleep.

"I ENTRUST YOU WITH MY CHILD"

ARNIE:	Today is September 7, 1998, and it is a very special day for our family.
RUTH:	It is also a day of mixed emotions: sadness, joy, worry, anxiety, and excitement. It is the day we receive our new daughter into our family.
JEANNIE:	This is the hardest decision I have ever made—to give my daughter, Brett, to you to be raised in your home. I am doing this because I want her to have a good life because I love her with all my heart.
ARNIE:	We know this day is hard for you and we respect the struggle you have had to arrive at this point.
RUTH:	I am glad we have an open-adoption agreement so that Brett will know who you are. While Brett is coming here to be our daughter, she will always be your daughter, too.
JEANNIE:	I want Brett to know I did this so that she will have a good life and a good family that will love her. She will have the things she needs to grow. At this time I pass Brett over to you. (Ruth takes Brett)
RUTH:	I promise to be the best mother I can be. I also promise that she will know the love you have for her. She will know that from us and from the letters you send. (Ruth passes Brett to Arnie)
ARNIE:	I promise to be the best father I can be. I also promise that she will know the respect we have for you for your decision.
RUTH:	You did not give Brett a middle name when she was born. We would like to do that now. Arnie's sister Thelma died earlier this year and we would like to give Brett her name as her middle name.
ARNIE:	Thelma was a special person. She was strong, happy, optimistic, and excited about life. We have these wishes for Brett as we add this name as her middle name.
JEANNIE:	So now Brett Ulitsky will be known as Brett Thelma

	Lyman. That is a good name. Decisions about Brett are now up to you. I believe you will make good decisions.
ARNIE:	We will try our best.
RUTH:	Thank you for trusting us to take care of Brett. I promise you we will treasure her.
JEANNIE:	And I treasure both of you.
Group hug	

AFTERWARDS

Even though they had come to know each other and had said these same words many times, the finality of the moment was very emotional. They had decided earlier to keep the camera rolling when they became emotional. They believe that when any of them look at the video in years to come, alone or with Brett, seeing their feelings expressed will be important to show that they all understood the intensity of the moment. They had been able to put together an agreement with which all were happy in terms of future contact, so they knew that this was a beginning, as well as an ending. When the ceremony was over, the social worker drove Jeannie home and talked with her. Ruth and Arnie joyfully took their now-awake daughter home.

SITUATION

An adopted infant is introduced to the birth children.

Naomi and Herman, who had two biological children—Winnie, age four, and Robin, age six, decided to add another child through adoption. They were called late at night and told that they had to be at the airport the next day to pick up a son who was being escorted from Lithuania. Naomi and Herman were overwhelmed and felt that their children, while receptive to the adoption, would also be overwhelmed by the lack of time to prepare. They had planned a ceremony but needed to modify it to help their children. Two hours before they left for the airport, they did Part I, and within 20 minutes of arriving home, they did Part II.

	"A NEW ADDITION IS COMING"

MOMMY:	We have talked to you about adopting a little boy from Lithuania. When we talked, you said you were excited about having a brother.
DADDY:	This little boy needs to be adopted into a family that can take care of him. His first mother and father could not take care of him and left him in an orphanage.
MOMMY:	An orphanage is a place that takes care of children abandoned by their parents until a new family can be found. They found us to adopt Milton and be his family forever.
DADDY:	When we talked to you, we said we did not know how long it would be before your brother would join us. It could be fast or slow. Do you remember that? (Waits for each to answer)
MOMMY:	We got a call last night. And guess what the person said. She said that your brother was going to fly here today. What do you think? (Waits for each to answer)
DADDY:	We got a phone call late last night telling us the baby would be coming on a plane tonight. In a little while, we are going to the airport to get your brother. Granny is coming over to stay with you. Sometimes planes get delayed and it might be late before we get home. But tonight is special, so even if you fall asleep, we will wake you up to see your brother.
MOMMY:	This is now the time in the ceremony when you get to ask questions and tell us your thoughts, feelings, and ideas. (Time is taken for discussion. In this case, the girls wanted to make decorations to welcome their brother home. Their parents reminded them that their new brother's name would be Milton and showed them how to spell it. They also promised that after the ceremony was over they would help

their daughters find materials to use to make their decorations.)

DADDY: Part I of our ceremony is over. The next time we get into our family circle, Milton will be part of this family.

Hugs

The parents returned from the airport by 8:00 p.m. with Milton, who was asleep. Both girls were awake and anxious to see their new brother. The parents talked about how special the decorations were. After a few minutes of settling in, they started Part II.

"A NEW ADDITION HAS ARRIVED"

(Granny holds the baby in the circle so that the girls can have their parents' full attention)

DADDY: This is the moment we have been waiting for—Milton's joining our family.

MOMMY: We want to know how you feel right now.
(Waits for responses—which were happy and excited)

DADDY: We are glad that you feel that way right now. We do, too. We want you to know some important things. First, every time a new child comes into a family, a parent's love gets bigger. That way, every child keeps and gets all the love they need.

MOMMY: Second, you may feel lots of things later. You may feel happy and mad at the same time. You may be glad he is here and upset that he is here. We understand that you can have all these feelings and we want you to know we love you and all your feelings.

DADDY: Third, because Milton is so little, he will need a lot of attention. You need attention, too, so let us know if you aren't getting enough. Okay?
(Waits for responses from both children)

MOMMY: What would you like to say to us and Milton right now?

	(Waits for responses)
DADDY:	When Milton cries, he will need help from Mommy and me. If you hear him cry tonight, don't worry. We will take care of what he needs. If he wakes you up, try to go back to sleep.
MOMMY:	Always remember that we love you and are here for you, too.
Hugs	

AFTERWARDS

For the first few nights, Milton cried a lot until he got used to his new surroundings. The girls became irritated at times and told their parents, who accepted their feelings without judgment. In general, the transition seemed easier for their daughters than they had expected.

NONVERBAL ALTERNATIVES: TRANSITIONS

In a child's life, there will be people who die and whom they will never see again. Other people, such as the biological parents, may be out of physical contact but they might see them again. In addition, the adoption has brought new people into their lives. The purpose of mapping all this out is to help the child gain perspective. Instead of words, you can have photographs or drawings representing these people. You then take four large sheets of paper. At the top of one sheet, put a sad—even crying—face to represent the people who have died. At the top of the next sheet, put a face that is half sad and half smiling to represent the people who are out of the picture physically right now, but whom the child might see again. The last two sheets (or more if needed) would have smiling faces representing the people who are now in the child's life. Children will lose interest if the ceremony takes too long, so you might gather the pictures ahead of time. Together with the child, you could decide where to put the pictures. You can always return to this list and add to it later if the child wants to. Remember, the ceremony is to help the child and not to make sure that every possible person in the child's world is on the sheet of paper.

Even if children do not understand spoken English, they might relate to pictures in a book that show new children coming into the family and the range of emotions with which one might respond to them. Children could also point to expressions on faces on posters to indicate how they feel and a parent could make the same face to indicate that he or she understands. One might also write words describing the expressions so the child can begin to associate the expressions with words.

When children have been out of the home for reasons that are less than positive, they need to know that they are still welcome in the family. Are they still loved and accepted? If the words are not clear, use hugs, smiles, loving looks, reassuring pats, head stroking, back rubs, or cuddling. Anything that assures a child that he or she is still loved and a part of the family is important. Remember that appropriate discipline and limit setting are also ways of showing love and acceptance.

To represent transitions, it is often good to have a starting place, a bridge, and a resulting place. A key concept to teach is that for every ending, there is a beginning of one kind or another. You could actually make a bridge out of a cardboard box or use masking tape on the floor, carpet, or sidewalk to represent the start; two parallel rows to represent the sides of a bridge; and another marked area for the destination. This pattern could be used for children who are moving to new classrooms, homes, schools, responsibilities, privileges, and so on.

✑ 4 ✎

Ceremonies to Bolster Self-Esteem

> *"Making Room for Good Messages"*
> *"Feeling Good About Being You"*
> *"There Is a Place Here for Both of Us"*

ISSUES OF SELF-ESTEEM are closely tied to adoption. The act of being given up by the biological parents implies to the children that they are at fault in some way. As they internalize this viewpoint, they continually collect evidence to support it. Moves to and from different foster homes or back and forth among biological family members create damaged egos. By the time these children are placed in an adoptive home, they may genuinely believe that they are bad, worthless people. Often their behavior causes reactions that reinforce their negative self-images. Years of reinforcement make it difficult to dislodge these images, and simply telling a child that he or she is okay will not work.

The "Making Room for Good Messages" ceremony can be a powerful exercise for change. In this ceremony, the negative words remembered by the child can be written down and then destroyed while new, positive words are recorded in a scrapbook to be constantly referred to for reinforcement.

The "Feeling Good About Being You" ceremony reinforces the rights of the child to have needs and to be himself or herself and speaks of the love of the parents for the child. The permanence of this love for all the children in the family is the focus of the "There Is a Place Here for Both of Us" ceremony.

~

SITUATION
Trying to shift a child's negative behavior pattern.

After 10-year-old Matthew was officially adopted by Darcy and Judah, it was time to set up a meeting with his birth parents (court-mandated open adoption). There had been visits with his biological brother in another foster home, and it was decided that the families would meet at a Department of Social Services office. The session was difficult for everyone. The finality of the moment was overwhelming for Matthew, who realized that he would never be going back to live with his birth mother, and this visit where he said goodbye with no hope of returning was devastating. For people who do not understand why a child would want to go back to a house where abuse and neglect were rampant, the situation might be compared to the witness protection program. The government promises you safety. All you have to do is give up everything that has been part of your life so far. It must be very difficult to accept that offer.

Matthew's upset continued and finally resulted in his being suspended from school and after-school programs. He expressed no remorse, and often said that he didn't care about anything. His adoptive parents were stumped, and when it was suggested they do a ceremony, they decided that they had nothing to lose.

"MAKING ROOM FOR GOOD MESSAGES"

PREPARATION

Take several 3 × 5 index cards and put a bad message on each one. The messages should be based on knowledge of what had been said to the child in his or her past and what the child has said aloud about himself or herself.

- You are a rotten kid.
- You'll be the death of me yet.
- You'll never make it.
- You are unlovable.
- You are stupid.
- You are dumb.
- You are bad.

- You drive me crazy.
- You are a monster.
- You are clumsy.
- I hate you.
- Why can't you be good like (name)?
- It is your fault that you can't live here.

Then get another group of index cards. Cut each card into an interesting shape and put a colorful sticker on it. The messages used for Matthew were:

- You are good.
- You have a nice smile.
- You are unique.
- You try to do your best.
- You are super.
- You are huggable.
- You are lovable.
- You are smart.
- You are a terrific kid.
- You are kind.
- You have courage.
- You are special.
- You are brave.
- You are willing to try new things.
- You will be the best you can be.
- You are wonderful.
- You are helpful.
- You are clever.

The good messages should focus on basic characteristics, not on things the child did or did not do, such as, "You are good in math" or "You don't mess up your room." For Matthew's ceremony, two colorful folders were attached in such a way that the inside had three sections—enough to hold the good messages. The outside was decorated with colorful stickers and "Matthew's Good Messages" was printed on the front cover.

Also at hand were Scotch tape and a glue stick (so Matthew would have a choice later) and a small, reclosable plastic bag.

THE CEREMONY

MAMA:	Everyone at some time will hear good messages and bad messages from people.
PAPA:	Sometimes people say good things, such as, "You are a nice person." Sometimes people say bad things, such as, "You are a rotten person."
MATTHEW:	People might be kidding around and say things like, "Boy was that dumb," and you may feel like they said you were really dumb. That kind of kidding hurts. Sometimes people are angry or tired and they can say things like, "I could kill you" or "You are a monster." Children can take those messages and have them grow inside of them so that soon they believe that they are bad or rotten or no good.
PAPA:	What kids have to learn is that just because people say bad messages, that does not make them true. Because kids are small and growing, they may not have room for good messages unless we get rid of the bad messages from time to time.
MAMA:	Today's ceremony will do just that—get rid of bad messages so that there can be room for more good ones. Matthew, are you ready to do that now?
MATTHEW:	(Says his answer. If Yes, go on; if No, stop for the time being and do this ceremony later.)
IF THEY CONTINUE:	
MAMA:	We have written on cards bad messages that adults and other kids sometimes give kids. If you have ever had that bad message given to you, let us know and we will put that into a pile.
PAPA:	If you can remember a time you heard it or a person who said it and want to share that, we will listen. If you have gotten messages that we have not written on cards, let us know and we will add them to the pile. After we do this, Mama will explain what happens to the bad messages.

(Matthew reads each message and puts some of them in a pile. When he is done, he decides to put all of them into a pile, just in case someone said one of these and he doesn't remember. Then Papa asks him to read each card out loud and then to tear each into tiny pieces and put all the pieces into the reclosable plastic bag. Papa closes the bag, has Matthew stomp on it, and then throws it into the trash. Since Matthew was having trouble with fire setting, they decided not to burn these messages. Matthew walks back, saying how much room he has for good messages.)

MAMA: Now that we have started to remove the bad messages and there is room for good messages, we need to fill that space. We have written on cards good messages that we think apply to you. If you agree, we will make a way to push them into the space you now have for them. After each message is chosen and absorbed, we will put them in a special folder so that you can look at them often and share them with others.

(Mama shows Matthew the cards and he reads each of them, stopping to enjoy the stickers, too. He says he likes the stickers and doesn't want to eat them to get them inside. Mama assures him that he does not have to. They decide that Matthew will pick up each card in turn and Mama and Papa will read it. Matthew will put it next to his body at his head, his upper chest, or his abdomen. Mama and Papa will read it together and pretend to push it into his body at one of the three places he chooses. Then Matthew puts each card aside. Halfway through, Matthew throws his arms wide open and with a big smile says, "I am being so filled up with good messages." Papa shows Matthew the folder and helps Matthew put his cards inside the folder—this is not rushed, but done at Matthew's pace.)

MATTHEW: (Says how he feels now and what he thinks of the ceremony. Then he reads.) It is important for me to hold these good messages inside me. If I ever feel as though bad messages are trying to push them out, I will let you know that I need another ceremony to help me. I promise to try to believe the good messages people give me and to learn to manage the bad.

PAPA: We promise to help you hold on to good messages. If I ever give you bad messages that hurt you inside, please tell me so that I can change those messages right away.

MAMA:	If I ever give you bad messages that hurt you inside, please tell me so that I can change those messages right away.
PAPA:	We will end the ceremony by reading the good messages in your folder because we believe they are all true.
	(Mama and Papa read each message in turn.)
Group hug	

AFTERWARDS

At one point in the ceremony, Matthew threw his arms open and exclaimed, "I am really getting filled up with good messages!" His demeanor and behavior changed significantly after this ceremony. He stopped being oppositional and quieted down a lot. The ceremony had helped him cross a bridge from despair back to calm. It seemed to be one of the most behavior-changing events in this child's life.

SITUATION

A child has low self-esteem.

After Wilma and Nick adopted eight-year-old Juanetta, things seemed to go pretty smoothly until the child started saying, "I am dumb," or "I am stupid," or "I am ugly." They asked her whether the kids had been teasing her. She said No, but that she felt she wasn't as good as the other kids. Nothing Wilma and Nick said seemed to make any difference. Whenever she made a mistake or didn't know the answer to something, she would start her self-deprecating statements. Since Juanetta was not paying attention to her parents, it was suggested that they put together a ceremony, as the "formalizing" of the comments might help them be heard and remembered better.

"FEELING GOOD ABOUT BEING YOU"

DADDY:	Some people think that children have to behave a certain way in order to be okay. Other people believe that children are okay simply for being who they are.

MOMMY:	We tell children how we expect them to behave and feel about themselves by what we say to them and about them.
JUANETTA:	As I was growing up, I heard lots of messages— some of them good and some bad. This ceremony is to help me remember that I am okay just because I am me.
MOMMY:	The first thing we want to say is that we are glad you exist.
JUANETTA:	I have a right to grow and to become the best person I can be.
DADDY:	We look forward to helping you grow and watching you become the best person you can be. We also want to say that your needs are okay with us.
JUANETTA:	That means that it is okay for me to need things. You are here to help me with my needs.
MOMMY:	Yes, we understand that you have needs because we have needs, too. We are here to help you with what you need.
DADDY:	We are glad you are a girl.
JUANETTA:	That does not mean that girls are better than boys. It means that you both are glad that I am me.
MOMMY:	We appreciate who you are. We are glad you are who you are. We like to hold you.
JUANETTA:	That means that I am a lovable person who deserves to be held and hugged as much as I want to be.
DADDY:	There are lots of ways to let you know you are lovable—smiles, hugs, kisses, handshakes, listening to you, sharing something important. People need these things to grow.
JUANETTA:	Those are some of the ways I let you know you are lovable, too.
MOMMY:	That's right. I feel very lucky to be your mommy. I like you just because you are you.
DADDY:	And I feel very lucky to be your daddy. I like you just because you are you.
JUANETTA:	So I need to remember that: You are glad I am here.

My needs are okay with you.
You are glad I am me.
I am a lovable person and you like to hold me.

DADDY AND MOMMY: That is correct.
Group hug

AFTERWARDS

While Juanetta still expressed feelings of being stupid, her complaints became less frequent, and less intense, as well.

~

SITUATION

Reassuring children that there is room for all of them in the family.

The agency that helped Cheri in the adoption of her first son asked her if she would consider taking the boy's younger, biological brother, who was unable to remain in his preadoptive home. Cheri said she needed time to think about it. After considering all the pros and cons, she recognized that the bottom line was that the two boys were brothers. Cheri had had one sister, who died at age 36 of ovarian cancer. They had been the best of friends, and she wanted the boys to have that same chance to be with each other as brothers should be. She had never written a song before, but did so during a weekend retreat of music she attended. In its lyrics was her answer. She tried singing it to the boys, but they were not interested. Then, when issues of concern started to loom extra large, she decided to turn the lyrics into a ceremony.

"THERE IS A PLACE HERE FOR BOTH OF US"

MAMA: My lap has room for two
               No matter what you say or do
               You'll grow up and get tall
               Off my lap you'll not fall
               My lap has room for two.

ERIC: And we will be a family
               Through all the bad and good

CHRIS: Forever we'll be
               Chris, Eric,

MAMA:	And me.
ALL:	For all our whole lives through
MAMA:	My arms have hugs for two.
CHRIS:	No matter what we say or do
ERIC:	Hugs get better as we see
	What each person needs.
MAMA:	My arms have hugs for two.
CHRIS:	And we will be a family
ERIC:	Through all the bad and good
	Forever we'll be
CHRIS:	Chris, Eric, and
MAMA:	Me.
ALL:	For all our whole lives through
MAMA:	My heart has love for two.
ERIC:	No matter what we say or do
	Love will grow—there's no doubt.
CHRIS:	It will never run out.
MAMA:	My heart has love for two
ERIC:	And we will be a family.
CHRIS:	Through all the bad and good
	Forever we'll be
MAMA:	Chris, Eric, and me.
ERIC:	For all our whole lives through.
MAMA:	And my sons, you will learn this, too.
	And my sons, you will learn this, too.
	And my sons, you will learn this, too.
	As I give, you see, it comes back to me
	My love just grows and blooms.
ALL:	And we will be a family
	Through all the bad and good.
	Together we'll be Chris, Eric, Mommy,
	For all our whole lives through.

Group hug

AFTERWARDS

The boys loved this ceremony. They seemed to get into the repetition of ideas and lines. Even though they did not listen to it as a song, they seemed to connect with it as a ceremony. They repeated parts of it for weeks afterward.

NONVERBAL ALTERNATIVES: SELF-ESTEEM

Children became used to receiving stars and other stickers in school. Teachers continue to give them out because children respond well. From time to time, you might present simple and colorful awards to your child for being kind, having a nice smile, comforting a sad person, cleaning his room especially well, learning to ride her bike without training wheels, and so on.

You can take time to provide verbal recognition for doing well: "Thank you for being so patient," "You certainly are clever," "You have a good eye for color," or "What you said is very interesting." Also take time to make positive statements to your child, especially when your remarks are unexpected and not tied to any achievement: "I'm lucky to know you"; "I like you"; "It's good to see you"; "I love you"; "Thanks for being you"; "I'm glad you're here"; "I enjoy being with you." Look into your child's eyes when you say these things. The members of one family, for example, used a Sunday lunch time, when the family was usually together after church, to describe one thing they appreciated about each person in the family each week. They kept the rules for speaking simple: say only positive things; be serious, and don't make jokes; try to be specific; and only say things that are true from each person's perspective. The listening rules were also simple: listen carefully to what each person says; don't joke or put yourself down; enjoy what you hear. They even found a way to include very young children. Someone might say, "I like the way you try to feed yourself," or if spoken language was still a problem, they would use a special smile or touch or voice tone for that person—still always remembering to use eye contact.

If you have more than one child, rotate the honor of being child of the day. The child of each day gets to choose the book that is read at night and has his or her picture put in a frame labeled "Child of the Day." That way, every child in a family with more than one child gets his or her chances to feel special and singled out.

❧ 5 ❧

Ceremonies for Loss

> *"I Can Care"*
>
> *"Rejection and Abandonment"*
>
> *"Goodbye–Hello"*
>
> *"Saying Goodbye to Our Old Home"*
>
> *"Saying Hello to Our New Home"*
>
> *"What Is Going to Happen Now?"*
>
> *"Sparky's Memorial Service"*

LOSS IS A part of our daily lives. We lose loved ones when they die, move away, or end the relationship. For children adopted as infants, the loss of the biological parents is a mystery that raises questions for them throughout their lives. For the child adopted at an older age, this is often the latest step in a series of family disconnections. These children may have spent a part of their lives with one or both parents, extended family members, and/or foster parents. Each move adds to the sadness at the separation and creates fear of the unknown future. Most often, these feelings are not expressed. It may be difficult for the new family to deal with a child's grief so there is little motivation to acknowledge the child's sadness. In fact, it is natural for families to do their best to cheer up the grieving child. The child's feelings then go underground, only to surface in the future as problematic behaviors, such as withdrawal, self-destruction, aggression, and depression.

Very often, feelings of loss turn into anger. The loss of control is an uncomfortable feeling, and the child will search for ways to re-exert control over his or her feelings. One way to counteract these helpless feelings might be to act out, or rage, against someone or something. A family dealing with an angry child may well look to what other feelings are being covered up. Ceremonies that allow for an expression of feelings may alleviate the need to act out anger.

Ceremonies that deal with loss are a way to name the sad and fearful and angry feelings, make them acceptable and normal, and give the child permission to express them. The "I Can Care" ceremony approaches the subject of loss in a general way. It helps children to understand the concept, connect it to themselves, and consider how they feel about losing someone or something close to them. It also offers the promise of hope for reconnecting with new people and things.

The "Rejection and Abandonment" ceremony deals specifically with the loss of birth parents. It allows the adoptive parents to acknowledge the significance of this loss for their child. It also relates the specific problem behavior that reflects the feelings of rejection and the fear of future abandonment, and can help the child better understand the connection.

"Goodbye–Hello" ceremonies are useful as children move from one family to another; move, with their family, to a new home; or change schools, teachers, social workers, or therapists. Such ceremonies as "Sparky's Memorial Service" can be created to focus on the loss and not on the replacement when one is dealing with the death of a family member, a friend, or a pet, and requires time to mourn.

"Saying Goodbye to Our Old Home" and "Saying Hello to Our New Home" are ceremonies written specifically to assist an adopted child with a move. Because many adopted children experience multiple moves without preparation, these ceremonies are especially helpful in establishing a new pattern that will engender trust in the parents and comfort in the transition.

⌒

SITUATION
Facing the pain of loss and naming it so that a child can break a pattern of detachment.

Beth and Fred had been parents to their adoptive son, Ralph, for two years. Now nine years old, he had started behaving badly toward people and things. He would have a temper tantrum and break toys—even those he especially loved. He maintained that he didn't care if he hurt someone's feelings. When he lost something he loved, he would respond, "I don't care. I never liked it anyway." Since there seemed to be no way to connect with Ralph and his pain, Beth decided that a ceremony might help him by at least bringing his pain into the open. Perhaps if he could name it, he could find new ways to handle it.

"I CAN CARE"

DAD:	When you live in the world, there are times when the people you care about go away or things that you like are lost.
MOM:	At those times, you can feel like you never want to get attached to anyone or anything ever again.
RALPH:	You may meet someone and try very hard not to like them in case they go away or you go away. Or you may be given a present and you try hard not to care about it in case you lose it or someone takes it.
MOM:	It is natural to feel afraid of caring for short periods of time.
RALPH:	Feeling that way for a long time is not good.
DAD:	Maybe people have felt like they never belonged any place, or maybe, like children in foster homes, they never feel anything was really theirs.
RALPH:	If you feel things are temporary, you may learn not to care.
DAD:	But once you get adopted, things are permanent, which means forever.
RALPH:	The people in your life are your family forever.
MOM:	People give you toys that are yours to enjoy forever.
RALPH:	People help you get things that you want to play with. These are things that you can get attached to. They are for you. They are not temporary.
MOM:	And people like you and love you.
RALPH:	They are your family forever—not until the next family—but forever. No matter what you say or do, they are your family forever.
DAD:	So, now that things are forever, what do you need to do?
RALPH:	I can become attached. I can learn to take care of things because I am part of a permanent family.
MOM:	That's right.
RALPH:	I can become attached to people. I can care about people and their feelings.
DAD:	Sometimes we lose things we like or care about.

RALPH: When that happens, we feel sad.

MOM: At the same time, we need to remember that be-
                  cause we cared, we also felt happy and good in-
                  side.

RALPH: We all deserve to care and be cared about.

MOM FIRST, THEN RALPH:

                  One of the things I care about is _____
                  If I lost it, I would feel _____
                  And I would try to remember how much I enjoyed
                  having it.

DAD FIRST, THEN RALPH:

                  One of the people I care about is _____
                  If _____ever went away, I would feel ____
                  and I would remember how much I enjoyed know-
                  ing _____and try, if possible, to keep in
                  touch.

MOM: Life is so full of chances to care and feel the good
                  things that go with it. We care about you.

DAD: Yes, we do care about you.

RALPH: And I care about you.

ALL: We all care about each other.

Hug time

AFTERWARDS

*After the ceremony, Ralph stopped breaking his toys, which he had often done
deliberately. Although he still would have problems when he lost something, he
started to show more affection for Beth and Fred. They decided later that he
had started to let himself feel more connected to them than he had in the past.*

~

SITUATION
To help name and legitimize a painful issue.

*Staci and Leon adopted two siblings, Chan and Lai, at the same time, and they
had been living together as a family for four years. The adoption had been an
open one, mandated by the court, which Staci and Leon accepted happily. The two
children visited their birth mother (the birth father had dropped out of sight) three
times a year. About eight months earlier, the birth mother remarried and she and*

her new spouse decided to move 2,000 miles away. Both children began to reexperience rejection and abandonment. Their behavior at home was becoming more testy by the week. Staci and Leon asked for help in putting together a ceremony to help them all discuss the issues. They had tried talking to their daughter and son, but had met with silence. Lai was 14 and Chan was 11.

"REJECTION AND ABANDONMENT"

MOM:	This ceremony is about something we do not talk about although it is very important.
DAD:	This ceremony is about rejection and abandonment. Both of these are big words and very important words.
LAI:	Every adopted child feels rejected and abandoned by birth parents. No matter who comes along to take care of her, these feelings of being left never go away.
CHAN:	Adopted kids think about their first mom a lot. They grew inside her and they lived with her but they can't live with her any longer.
LAI:	Even if they believe they do not think about these feelings, every kid does.
CHAN:	Not living with your birth mother is a big loss—one of the biggest ever.
LAI:	Some kids act out in angry ways. These kids need to be in control. They lie and steal. They hide their feelings behind their behavior.
CHAN:	Other kids are more quiet with their pain. These kids try to please adults and are not always true to what they feel. They hide their feelings, too.
LAI:	What all these kids do not know is that they have a right to feel angry and sad about being rejected and abandoned by their old mom, and they can still love her, too.
CHAN:	Both kids who behave badly and those who be-have too well are troubled. They have trouble be-lieving that their adoptive parents also will not

	reject and abandon them, no matter what the parents say.
LAI:	I feel worried that when you go away, you will not come back.
CHAN:	I do not worry so much on the outside, but sometimes I worry on the inside.
MOM:	We know that both of you worry and we want to make some promises to you. I promise never to reject you even if I get so angry at what you do or say that I feel like exploding. Even if I get that angry, remember that I still love you. Let's shake on this. (Mom and kids shake hands.)
DAD:	I promise never to abandon you even if I get so annoyed that I feel like I need space from you and you might feel like you need space from me. Let's shake on this. (Dad and kids shake hands.)
CHAN:	You will understand that the feelings we have are okay.
MOM AND DAD:	Yes, we will.
LAI:	Sometimes we might yell and sometimes we might not do as we are told.
MOM AND DAD:	Yes, this will be your home no matter what you say or feel.
LAI:	Sometimes we might feel that we hate you and want to live with our old parents.
MOM AND DAD:	Yes, we know, and this will still be your home.
CHAN:	Thinking about this hurts.
MOM AND DAD:	Yes, and healing the pain is possible. We are all in therapy to help us.
CHAN:	We will go forward together.
LAI:	Feelings are okay—all feelings. We will learn to talk about them more.
MOM AND DAD:	Yes, let the healing continue.
Family hug	

AFTERWARDS

Lai and Chan responded extremely well to the ceremony, after which both children had a good cry. It gave them another way to express their upset over their loss in the short term. Over the long term, rejection and abandonment continue as issues.

⌒

SITUATION
A change of social workers.

The social worker assigned to work with eight-year-old Freda's placement later stepped in to help Freda's adoptive family with postadoption concerns. It proved to be a negative experience for the parents, Bernie and Ethan. Pat, the social worker, was very inexperienced and would express worry and dismay over how the parents handled things. She increased their stress level instead of supporting them. Bernie and Ethan wanted better support, and asked the agency to assign Ricki to work with them. She had done their home study and was the kind of person they believed could help them. The agency agreed to the change. The next step was to help Freda with the transition. Losing a social worker, even though the relationship had been a brief one, represented yet another loss in Freda's life. A ceremony was put together to help Freda face the loss, to help her say the words involved, and to help her realize that when people say goodbye, they often say hello to something or someone else.

When the two social workers came to the house, Freda went to her room and refused to come out. When she was told she was needed for a special ceremony, her curiosity got her out of her room.

"GOODBYE–HELLO"

DADDY:	Life is full of goodbyes and hellos. There are many kinds. Most goodbyes are for short times and may mean, "See you again soon" or "Talk to you again soon."
PAPA:	Some goodbyes are hellos, too. In Israel, people say "Shalom," which means goodbye and hello at the same time. Tonight we are having a special "Goodbye–Hello" ceremony.
PAT:	My name is Pat. I helped Freda find her forever home and family. I am happy that I helped bring all of you together. It is now time for me to say good-

	bye, but I will see you again. So goodbye and see you again. (Shakes the family members' hands.)
RICKI:	My name is Ricki. I helped Bernie and Ethan find Freda. I am happy that I helped bring Freda and her new parents together. It is now time for me to say a new hello—hello to all of you. I will be visiting with you and help you to be the best family you can be. (Shakes the family members' hands.)
FREDA:	My name is Freda. Today I say, "Goodbye, Pat, see you again. Thank you for helping Papa and Daddy find me. Hello, Ricki. When you visit, we can talk and play and go places. You will be our social worker and our friend."
Group hug	
DADDY:	Our "Goodbye–Hello" ceremony is now over.

AFTERWARDS

After the ceremony, Freda skipped outside and played. The next time she saw Ricki, Freda was friendly.

⌒

SITUATION
Saying goodbye to a former home.

Serena, a single adoptive mother, had just purchased her first home. She was excited about moving to a place of her own, but she knew that her six-year-old daughter, Kim Lee, would not feel the same. Kim Lee had been in so many foster homes that the idea of moving would be terrifying. Serena wanted Kim Lee to understand that they were a family no matter where they lived. She also wanted to convey that "home" was where the family lived together—not a specific place. She planned two ceremonies: one to say goodbye to the old home and one to say hello to the new home. Kim Lee was not a strong reader, so Serena helped her with any words with which she had trouble. Muffin was their cat and Buckley was a dog in their new neighborhood.

"SAYING GOODBYE TO OUR OLD HOME"

KIM LEE: Today is the day that we say goodbye to this home.

MAMA: This is the place where we first lived as a family.

KIM LEE: Even though we are leaving this home, we are still a family. Even when I grow up and go to live in my own house or apartment, we will still be a family.

MAMA: We liked these walls and floors. We liked these steps and carpets.

KIM LEE: We liked our rooms and bathrooms. We liked the backyard.

MAMA: We need to remember that the move may be hard for Pepper, too.

KIM LEE: We need to help her get used to her new home. Our being there will help.

MAMA: Our furniture and books and toys being there will help. She will still see some of the same people and she will probably meet new people.

KIM LEE: I wonder how she will feel about Buckley.

MAMA: So we say thank you, house, for being our home and giving us shelter and keeping us safe. We hope that the next people who live here enjoy being here.

KIM LEE: Goodbye, home, and thank you. We will miss you and we will remember you. We hope you will feel happy with your new family. We will enjoy our new home.

Hug time

AFTERWARDS

Leaving went smoothly. While Kim Lee did, at times, refer to their old home and how it was different from their new home, she settled in nicely.

SITUATION
Saying hello to a new home.

Since moving day was a Saturday and their new neighbors would be at home, Serena explained the ceremony to them and asked if they would like to be present. Both Joy and Clyde said they were delighted to be asked. In fact, Clyde helped Kim Lee put the mezuzah, a symbol that identifies a Jewish home, on the front door frame.

"SAYING HELLO TO OUR NEW HOME"

KIM LEE: This is the day we say hello to our new home. "Hello, new home."

MAMA: This is a special day. We have brought with us special things to help us say "Hello." These things are part of Jewish customs.

KIM LEE: The first thing we bring is bread. We bring this with a wish that we will always have enough to eat.

MAMA: The second thing is sugar. With this, we bring a wish that we will always have sweetness in our family when we live in this home.

KIM LEE: The third is salt. This reminds us that sometimes things are not so sweet—maybe even bitter. As a family, we have to learn to take the bitter with the sweet.

MAMA: The fourth is candles. With the candles comes a wish that we will always have light and joy in this home.

KIM LEE: Into this home we bring our memories of our last home. Most of all, we bring ourselves.

MAMA: Yes, and we are a very special family.

KIM LEE: And we have our furniture and toys and books and dishes.

MAMA: We also say hello to our two new neighbors and friends, Joy and Clyde.

KIM LEE:	Yes, we say hello to Joy and Clyde and to their dog, Buckley.
MAMA:	We will have fun saying a lot of new hellos.
KIM LEE:	And we have one last important thing to do.
MAMA:	We will put a mezuzah on our door. This is a way in which Jewish people bless a Jewish home. (The mezuzah is placed on the door.)
KIM LEE:	Our ceremony is complete, except for one final thing—a group hug.
Hug time	

AFTERWARDS

The ceremony was a moment of calm in the middle of chaos. It helped Kim Lee meet neighbors and feel connected to the place and the people. It also made the piled-up boxes seem less troublesome for Serena.

⌒

SITUATION
Parents with an adopted daughter decide to divorce.

Gretchen and Trevor had been married for six years when they adopted Amelia Gentle Wind, then two years old. When they decided to divorce six years later, they were able to work out their arrangements through mediation. Amelia would stay with her mother during the week, except for school vacation weeks, when she would stay with Trevor. Every other weekend, Amelia would stay with her dad, who was moving three miles away from the present home. Gretchen and Trevor wanted to make sure that Amelia understood that they loved her and were not divorcing her. They were sensitive to the fact that Amelia was about to lose yet another family. They already had talked with her about what was happening and the living arrangement. They felt that a ceremony would formally mark the change and help Amelia Gentle Wind with the loss and separation.

"WHAT IS GOING TO HAPPEN NOW?"

MOMMY: In just two days, our new way of living will start. We wanted to take a moment and have a ceremony to mark its beginning.

DADDY: On Saturday, I will be moving to my new apartment. I will not be living here anymore.

AMELIA: I know this is going to happen, and it makes me feel very sad.

MOMMY: We are sad, too. When people get married, they hope it will be for their whole lives. Sometimes things don't work out. When they don't, parents get a divorce.

DADDY: Parents divorce each other, but they never divorce their children. We still love you very much. We are sorry to do something that makes you sad.

AMELIA: I don't want this to happen. I am sad and angry, too.

MOMMY: We understand your wish and your feelings, and we want to help you as much as we can.

DADDY: You will have your own room in both homes. Each place will have clothes and toys for you, too. Most important, we will still be your parents and a part of your life. I will always be your daddy.

MOMMY: I will always be your mommy. That will never change.

AMELIA: You will both be my parents forever. That is important. No one is divorcing me.

DADDY: And remember that this divorce is not your fault. You did not do anything to cause it, and you cannot do anything to fix it, no matter how hard you want to or wish to.

AMELIA: This divorce is not my fault and nothing I say or do will get the two of you to live together again.

MOMMY: Sometimes, when parents are worrying about what they need, they may not notice what their child needs. So you must let us know what you need so that we can help you.

DADDY:	If we confuse you, please let us know. Mommy and I will talk to each other regularly to try to avoid problems. And you must let us know if we miss a problem from time to time.
AMELIA:	So if I get confused or think there is a problem, I am supposed to tell you right away.
MOMMY AND DADDY:	Yes, that is correct.
AMELIA:	So what do I need to remember?
MOMMY:	The divorce is not your fault.
DADDY:	We are not divorcing you. You will be our daughter forever.
MOMMY:	You can't fix it and make us a family the same way we were before.
AMELIA:	We are going to be a family in a new way.
DADDY:	Wherever you are, you can always call the other parent on the phone if you need to or want to.
AMELIA:	And I can feel lots of different feelings. I feel sad and mad now because I don't want this to happen.
MOMMY:	Remember, Amelia, we are here to help you.
DADDY:	And we will love you and you will be our daughter forever.

Family hug

AFTERWARDS

Throughout the ceremony, Amelia would feel sad and begin to cry. Her parents were in no hurry. They did not want to cover so many details that Amelia would lose the point, so they limited the issues they brought up and tried to plan a lot of repetition to help the ideas stick in Amelia's head. The ceremony was hard for all of them emotionally, especially when Amelia did not want to finish it. They persuaded her to stay because it was important. They assured her that they could take all the time they needed to take. They took the telephone off the hook so that they would not be disturbed by its ringing. The ceremony took about half an hour and seemed to help them all. When Amelia said goodbye to her dad, he repeated the messages for the ceremony to her. She was crying and was able to say that she already understood what he was saying.

SITUATION
Death of a pet.

Edgar, 13 years old, had been living with his adoptive mother, Marissa, for seven years. When he was in his last foster home, he had grown very fond of the family dog, who listened to everything Edgar said and slept with him at night. When the foster parents informed them that Sparky had died, Edgar and his mom talked about it, but Edgar kept bringing it up whenever he felt sad. Marissa suggested that they do a memorial service for Sparky since they had missed the funeral and hadn't had been able to say goodbye. Edgar jumped at the chance and Marissa told him to write down the 10 best things about Sparky (borrowing the idea from the book The Tenth Good Thing About Barney *by Judith Viorst [1971]), and she helped him get started. They went to their synagogue to make it more official.*

"SPARKY'S MEMORIAL SERVICE"

EDGAR:	This is a special memorial service for remembering Sparky.
MOM:	When Sparky died, Ira and Claudia buried him, but you never really had a chance to say goodbye.
EDGAR:	No, I didn't, and I really miss him.
MOM:	We have come to the synagogue today to have this ceremony to remember and honor Sparky because he was a good friend and companion to you.
EDGAR:	Judaism asks us a question: What if we had the opportunity to decide that nothing would ever die as long as nothing was ever born? That would mean that there would be no more babies or kids.
MOM:	There would be no more first loves or new ideas.
EDGAR:	When we miss someone, that sounds like a good idea, but if it were true, I would never have been born to know Sparky.
MOM:	So in the cycle of life, all living things die.
EDGAR:	It is important to remember all the things that were

special about each person. I have 10 things I remember about Sparky:

- He protected me.
- He stayed by my side.
- He was playful.
- He liked to watch me play Nintendo.
- We played fetch together.
- He would run beside me when I rode my trike in the backyard.
- He was very intelligent.
- He cuddled with me when I was sad.
- He greeted me when I came home from school.
- He slept with me at night when I needed the company.

MOM:	Edgar, those were wonderful things. Sparky was a special dog. Here are some other words from Judaism to say about Sparky. [See Stein, 1996]
BOTH:	In the rising of the sun and in its going down, we remember him.
	In the blowing of the wind and in the chill of *winter*, we remember him.
	In the opening of the buds and in the rebirth of *spring*, we remember him.
	In the blueness of the sky and in the warmth of *summer*, we remember him.
	In the rustling of the leaves and in the beauty of *autumn*, we remember him.
	In the beginning of the year and when it ends, we remember him.
EDGAR:	When we are weary and in need of strength, we remember him.
MOM:	When we are lost and sick at heart, we remember him.
EDGAR:	When we have joys we yearn to share, we remember him.
BOTH:	So long as we live, he too shall live, for he is now a part of us, as we remember him.
MOM:	Edgar, is there anything else you'd like to say?
EDGAR:	(answers)

MOM: Let's close our ceremony with the Kaddish.*
BOTH: (recite the Kaddish)
Family hug

AFTERWARDS

Edgar said he wondered where all the people were whom he had expected to come to the memorial service. Marissa told him that theirs was a private service. Edgar seemed happier afterwards. Sparky is still missed, but less intensely and constantly.

NONVERBAL ALTERNATIVES: LOSSES

If your family is moving from one place to another, you could use chalk on a sidewalk and mark one spot with a drawing of your house and put some of your child's important things near it, along with an empty box. At a place some distance from the first house, draw a picture of another house (if you only know one way to make a simple house, then use different colors). Your child can help pack the box and you can put the packed box into a wagon. Your child can then ride to the new house on a tricycle, for instance, while you pull the filled box and get there first. The child gets to the new house and sees his or her stuff there, helps to unpack it, and plays with the contents. If outdoors is not a possibility, you can put some chairs together as if you were in a car and pretend to be driving to the new house, where you see the filled box.

When you leave a home, saying goodbye is important. You could say the words and the child could wave goodbye to each part: "Goodbye, bathroom"; "Goodbye, basement"; "Goodbye, bedroom." Or you could say more if the child is older: "Goodbye bedroom. I felt safe here and had good dreams. I will take these good feelings to my new house." The child then waves goodbye. When you get to the new house, you reverse the process:: "Hello, new bedroom. You will be a safe room for me and one in which I will have good dreams. If I ever have unsafe feelings or bad dreams, Mommy and Daddy will help me." The child waves hello as you talk.

You could also take pictures of rooms in the present house and of those in the new house, if these rooms are empty (if the other family's furniture is still

---

*A Hebrew prayer said in remembrance of someone who died, it actually contains no references to death or dying, but allows a mourner to affirm the justice of God and the meaningfulness of life.

there, a child might be confused and think that it is your new family furniture). Put the pictures of the rooms in a folder or notebook. When you get to the new house, the child tries to identify the new rooms from the pictures. If you have two children, they can work together. If you have more than two children, they could work in groups, with the older ones paired with younger ones. Be sure not to make it a competition. One way to do that is to say that when all the teams are successful, there will be a prize for everyone. That should promote cooperation.

To focus on the divorce of adoptive parents, one could cut out pictures that clearly represent each person in the family. If parents are of the same gender, try to use color or a special characteristic to be sure the child knows which one is which. Then draw two places of residence—houses or apartments, as appropriate. Start by showing the family together and then show one parent's leaving for another home, and then the nonresidential parent and the child visiting. You might draw some hearts to show that love between parents and the child remains very big while that between the two parents is gone. You also need to demonstrate that the divorce is not the child's fault in any way. Perhaps part of the story is that the two parents decide that they need to divorce because they cannot live together as parents anymore as they do not get along. However, they still love the child and feel sad that they will hurt the child. When the story continues, they explain that they made a decision separate from the child because it was an adult problem to solve. Always make sure that the last piece shows the three together.

❧ 6 ❧

Ceremonies to Encourage Learning

> *"Life Is Full of Choices"*
> *"This Is Me, This Is Us"*
> *"Feelings"*

IT IS OFTEN noted that adopted children have difficulty learning. There are several possible reasons for this. For children born into multiproblem families, the birth mother may not have had prenatal care, proper nutrition, or a drug- and alcohol-free pregnancy, which can cause learning disabilities in the child. Also, for children who are preoccupied with safety and security, as may be the case for those separated from their birth families, the concentration necessary for learning may be a luxury they cannot afford. Betty Jean Lifton (1981), in her book *Lost and Found*, suggested that the closed and secretive nature of adoption, and the tendency of many adoptive parents to ignore the past, may give their children the message that it is best not to be curious, not to ask questions, and not to delve deeply into matters of interest, thus contributing to an antilearning stance.

Ceremonies can provide a way to encourage learning. The "Life Is Full of Choices" ceremony, the "This Is Me, This Is Us" ceremony, and the "Feelings" ceremony each takes a sophisticated concept that a parent might want to teach a child and puts it into a format that is participatory and relevant.

~

SITUATION
A birth child and an adopted child quarrel.

Larry and Josie had a birth daughter, Karyn, who was 10 years old when they adopted Paul, age seven. They had expected sibling squabbles, but were surprised at the intensity of the fighting and the lack of responsibility each child took for his or her own behavior. Karyn, who usually told the truth, kept saying that everything was Paul's fault. Paul, who had been in the family for one year, maintained that everything was Karyn's fault. In addition, they both started saying such things as, "She made me angry so I had to hit her" or "He made me do this." The parents wanted help in getting the message across to the kids that they had choices about what they did and how they reacted. They knew some fighting would continue and they wanted the children to realize that they had separate brains and could make choices in most situations in their lives.

"LIFE IS FULL OF CHOICES"

DAD:	Life is full of choices.
MOM:	We make choices every day.
KARYN:	We make choices every hour.
PAUL:	We make choices every minute.
MOM:	People make choices to tell the truth or tell a lie. I made a choice to always tell my family the truth. Sometimes that choice is hard for me, but I want you to know that you can trust me.
DAD:	Me, too. So I tell you the truth even if I sometimes do not look so good in doing it.
PAUL:	People also make choices about fighting. We can start a fight, continue a fight, or walk away. We make choices like this every day.
KARYN:	Sometimes, when we are tired, we fight more because we are not sure what else to do. We know that to fight or not to fight is a choice.
PAUL:	Some people make choices about listening. Some people choose to listen to what others say and some do not.

KARYN:	They make a choice to not listen, or daydream, or think of other things. To listen or not to listen is a choice.
DAD:	At times, it seems as though these are not choices. Mom and I cannot choose to stay home and play because our job is to work and take care of the family.
MOM:	We can choose to feel good about it most of the time. We love our work and enjoy taking care of our family.
KARYN:	Children also have choices. They can feel good or bad about doing a chore.
PAUL:	If you choose to feel good, you will probably enjoy what you are doing. If you choose to feel bad, you will probably hate what you are doing. Both are choices.
KARYN:	I can choose to try new things or not.
PAUL:	I can choose to obey the rules and stay safe or not. I have a lot of choices.
ALL:	Here is hoping that we all make the best choices that we can.

Group hug

AFTERWARDS

Karyn and Paul continued to blame each other for their choices and to hold onto the role of victim that they had enjoyed for so long. Their parents continued to point out to them when they had choices to make and which choice, and its consequence, they seemed to have preferred. It is a concept that many adults cannot accept, and one with which the children still have trouble.

$\sim$

SITUATION
Separation issues resurfacing at puberty.

One of the problems that face parents who have adopted older children surfaces at puberty. In addition to all the normal preadolescent issues, others lurk in the background. When children near the age of two, they learn that they can differentiate themselves—pull away and say "No" and still be part of a family.

Children in dysfunctional homes have not had an opportunity to challenge adults and become their own person and still know they are loved and are part of a family. Most children who are adopted when they are older come from unstable families. While pulling away is a hard task for adolescents in general, it can be overwhelming and terrifying for adopted children. Before problems started to surface, Elsie decided to do a ceremony that would explain the issue in a dramatic sense rather than as a lecture. She also wanted to include her second daughter, even though she was younger. Luann was 12½ years old and Rachel was 10.

"THIS IS ME, THIS IS US"

MAMA:	Life is full of opposites, full of pushes and pulls.
LUANN:	Sometimes you feel sad, sometimes you feel happy.
RACHEL:	Sometimes you like being with someone, sometimes you like being by yourself.
MAMA:	When kids are between the ages of one and three, they learn they can pull away and explore their uniqueness—their specialness as people.
RACHEL:	They also learn they can come in close and be taken care of and loved and supported at the same time.
LUANN:	When kids come from families where parents don't understand this, kids don't learn this.
RACHEL:	So some kids do not understand how to be their special selves and a close member of the family at the same time.
MAMA:	Why is this important to our family?
LUANN:	When we lived with our birth mom and dad, they did not know how to take good care of us.
RACHEL:	They did the best they could, but they did not know how to help us learn how we could be close and be separate at the same time.
MAMA:	This is something I can help you learn. In this family, you can try ways of becoming the best person you can be. And you can come in close and show you belong. Let's practice. Luann, you step away and say something that is true about you.
LUANN:	(Steps away and says something that is true about herself.)

MAMA:	Now come back and say something that is true about you in this family.
LUANN:	(Steps in and says something that is true about herself in this family.)
MAMA:	Rachel, you step away and say something that is true about you. Try to make it something different from what Luann said.
RACHEL:	(Steps away and says something that is true about herself.)
MAMA:	Now come back and say something true about you in this family.
RACHEL:	(Steps in and says something that is true about herself in this family.)
LUANN:	Okay, Mama, now you step away and say something that is true about you. (Mama does so.)
RACHEL:	Now come back and say something that is true about you in this family. (Mama does so)
MAMA:	The next thing to do is this: We will each take three steps back—one, two, three. Say "This is me. (This is me). Take three steps in—one, two, three. Say "This is us." (This is us.)
MAMA:	Let's do that two more times. (All do it.)
RACHEL:	We need to remember these ideas.
LUANN:	We can pull away and come close.
LUANN AND RACHEL:	We need to practice this some more until we learn it.
ALL:	(Step away and drop hands) This is me.
ALL:	(Step together and hold hands) This is us.
Group hug	

AFTERWARDS

The children needed a bit of coaching throughout the ceremony. Affirming who you are can be a difficult exercise. After this ceremony, for several weeks, they would stand at the dinner table and each would say, "This is me, this is us," before they sat down for dinner, just as reinforcement.

SITUATION
Trying to help a boy to express his feelings.

Simon, who had adopted 11-year-old Billy when he was nine, had done ceremonies with him almost from the beginning because he wanted to help Billy learn to express himself. Simon bought a poster that showed expressions on cartoon characters with corresponding labels of emotions, such as "furious," "silly," and "worried." He had been working with Billy to help him put words to how he felt, and lately the boy had been saying "I don't care" about most things. If someone hurt his feelings, he would say "I don't care." If he broke a rule and lost a privilege, he would say, "I feel fine." When he was told to take time out to cool off, he would deny feeling angry. This was Simon's attempt to legitimize Billy's feelings by making them worthy of a ceremony.

"FEELINGS"	

PAPA:	See if you can guess what I am thinking. Here are some clues. Everyone in the world has them. They can make your body feel tense or loose or jittery. They make people laugh and cry. Some are comfortable and some are uncomfortable. We can share them with other people or keep them wrapped up inside ourselves. Without them, life would be boring. What do you think these are?
BILLY:	Feelings. Everyone in the whole world has feelings. Some feelings, like anger, make your body feel tense. Some feelings, like happiness, can make your body feel loose. Some feelings, like nervousness, make your body feel jittery.
PAPA:	That's right. Some feelings are comfortable, like love and happiness. Some are uncomfortable, like fear and embarrassment.
BILLY:	Some people share their feelings with other people.

| | Some people try to hold all their feelings inside to try to pretend they are not there. |

PAPA: Some of the feelings kids have are:

  scared

  grateful

  hurt

  loved

  and warm

BILLY: Other feelings kids have are:

  worried

  silly

  hopeless

  brave

  confused

  and excited

PAPA: And people also use defenses. We use defenses. But if we use our defenses all the time, no one knows how we really feel or what we really need.

BILLY: Sometimes we need to use our defenses. But if we use our defenses all the time, no one knows how we really feel or what we really need.

PAPA: How do you protect your feelings sometimes? What do you look like when you are using your defenses? What do you say and do?

BILLY: When my feelings are hurt, but I don't want them to show, I look like this:

and I do or say this: _____

When I am worried but I do not want somebody to know, I look like this:

and I do or say

this: _____

When I am happy, but I don't want somebody to know, I look like this:

and I do or say

this: _____

PAPA: Thank you for sharing that. Since everything about feelings is important, let's see which of these ideas you believe is true. (Asks whether it is true or false

after each statement and waits for Billy to respond.*)

1. Every person in the world has feelings.
2. Feelings are not good or bad, they just *are.*
3. Some feelings are comfortable and some feelings are uncomfortable.
4. Sharing feelings can help us feel less lonely and afraid.
5. Sometimes we use defenses, such as ignoring or smiling on the outside, when we feel hurt.
6. Sometimes we need to use our defenses.
7. If we use our defenses all the time, no one knows how we really feel or what we need.
8. It is good to find people we trust with whom to share our feelings.
9. When we experience feelings, we feel more alive.
10. Papa loves me and all the feelings I have now or will ever have in the future.

Hug

AFTERWARDS

It is not clear whether or not this ceremony made a strong impression. Given the hope of the father that it would serve to reinforce the legitimacy of feelings, he assumed it did. No major changes were noticed as a result of the event.

NONVERBAL ALTERNATIVES: LEARNING

An excellent way to demonstrate that we are always making choices is to give a child a variety to choose among. In your ceremony, the child could have several choices:

- Do you want this piece of candy or that one? Child chooses.
- Do you want a hug or a kiss? Child chooses.
- Do you want to smile or to frown? Child chooses.

*Special note to parents: All of the statements are true.

- Do you want to skip or to hop? Child chooses.
- Do you want what is in this bag or is in that bag? Child chooses.

Then you can remind the child that we are always making choices. Some are easier to make than others. Remind the child that each time you make a decision, you have had choices. Try to make the best choices you can.

When you talk about feelings, you can use puppets with facial expressions. Your child can draw pictures showing feelings. You can draw faces and ask which one he or she feels like when happy, sad, mad, scared, or silly. You can say that all people have these feelings, and even more. As a parent, you can show which faces you feel and when. You can even ask if any feelings are missing, and if they are, perhaps the child can draw a face and show you another feeling. Ask the child when he or she felt this feeling. You might make up a story using all the faces, and then ask the child to try it as well. At the end, just remind him or her that everybody has feelings all the time. If we can tell people how we feel, they can help us if we need it. You could give an example: Someone who is sad might need a hug.

∂ 7 ∞

Ceremonies to Acknowledge Fears

> *"Monsters and Nightmares"*
>
> *"Going on Vacation"*
>
> *"This Is How I Feel Right Now"*
>
> *"You Are Safe Here"*

Fears are a normal part of childhood, and every age brings with it a range of fears for children to overcome. The ceremony for "Monsters and Nightmares" is a creative way to deal with these normal fears. However, there are other fears that can especially affect children who are adopted when they are older.

FEAR OF INTIMACY

After several moves, a child may become wary of placing his or her trust in a new family. The hurt and disappointment of investing one's feelings in parents, only to be uprooted in a move, is too devastating to repeat more than once or twice. Children learn to protect themselves by holding their feelings in check. They may say and do the "right" things, but emotionally they have placed a wall between themselves and their adoptive parents—and nothing can be more frustrating or sadder for the parents who have openly expressed their feelings toward the child.

A ceremony created to encourage small signs of caring, or the family hug that can be part of all ceremonies, is a starting point toward breaking down the wall. The "Coming, Going, and Staying" transitions ceremony also addresses the issue of holding back one's feelings for another person for fear of being hurt by the person's leaving.

FEAR OF REJECTION AND ABANDONMENT

These fears are common to adopted children as the separation from birth parents is interpreted as rejection. Adopted children tend to be exquisitely sensitive to signs of possible abandonment. The concept of a forever family needs to be reinforced both verbally and by concrete examples. Any separation from the adoptive parents is scary, even when the child may be doing something as pleasurable as visiting grandparents. The "Going on Vacation" ceremony directly addresses the child's fears that the parent(s) may not be there when the child returns.

The "This Is How I Feel Right Now" ceremony deals with the angst that underlies the fear of rejection and abandonment. The ceremony acknowledges the right of the child to feel angry and negative feelings, along with positive ones.

FEAR OF DISLOYALTY

For children who have known their birth parents, the memories can be very precious. Remembering can evoke the feelings of love the child had for them regardless of the difficulties they may have encountered as a family. These feelings of love are important to the child. As the child begins to feel attached to his or her adoptive parents, he or she may feel conflicted and disloyal to the birth parents. The "There Is Plenty of Room in a Heart," an anniversary ceremony (Chapter 8), can also be used here to help a child deal with his or her fear that if he or she loves the adoptive parents, the child will lose his or her love for the birth parents.

FEAR FOR ONE'S SAFETY

The "You Are Safe Here" ceremony deals in a forthright manner with the issue of the personal safety of a child. The Social Service community has become increasingly aware of the frequency of sexual abuse of children being placed in foster and adoptive homes. This ceremony allows this difficult subject to be openly addressed in order to assure the child that he or she can be secure in the new home.

~~

SITUATION

Being awakened nightly by a child frightened by nightmares and monsters.

Jasper, a single father, adopted Mohammed when the boy was five years old. When he was seven, the boy began to wake up nightly because of nightmares in which monsters chased him. Mohammed had been legally freed for adoption through a court battle. His parents had been abusive. Now that Mohammed was starting to feel safe and secure with Jasper, he was beginning to have hard nights. Jasper decided that the child must be remembering the terrible things that had happened to him, which meant that there was the hope of the start of a healing process. The problem was that Jasper had to get up early every morning to go to work, and being awakened every night was exhausting. The following ceremony was based on an idea from Cartoon Magic *by Richard J. Crowley and Joyce C. Mills (1989).*

PREPARATION

Jasper decided to use a whole sheet of flip-chart paper for large pictures and a half sheet for smaller ones. He also put together a variety of water-soluble markers (they don't go through the paper and are washable), as well as a pencil with an eraser and some crayons. That way, Mohammed could choose what he preferred to use. The first part of the ceremony was described on a sheet of paper. The rest of the ceremony—the action steps—was put on index cards. Jasper picked a floor space without carpeting.

"MONSTERS AND NIGHTMARES"	

DAD:	When I was a little boy, I was afraid of the dark. I would see shadows or hear noises and I would think they were monsters. Sometimes I had frightening nightmares that woke me up crying for help.
MOHAMMED:	Sometimes I am afraid of the dark. I see shadows or hear noises and I think they are monsters or ghosts or goblins. Sometimes I have frightening nightmares that wake me up crying for help.
DAD:	Today we are doing a ceremony for

MOHAMMED:	Monsters and nightmares.
DAD:	I am going to help you do some special things in order to master—that means be stronger than—those monsters and nightmares.
MOHAMMED:	I know that stronger means being stronger in my mind. It does not mean being big and grown up and tall. It means being strong in my head. You will help me do that today.
DAD:	Being strong in your mind may not happen all at once. But we will get started today. Are you ready to begin? If you answer No, we will stop the ceremony now and do it another time. If you answer Yes, we will continue.
MOHAMMED:	My answer is (If Yes, Dad starts handing Mohammed index cards, which he helps him read.)

STEP ONE

On one large sheet of paper, draw what your monsters look like. Talk about it a little.

STEP TWO

On another large sheet of paper, draw what one of your nightmares looks like. Talk about it a little.

STEP THREE

Look at your pictures and think of a cartoon character that you know is powerful enough to help you with your monsters and nightmares. Talk about who or what that is as you draw it on a large sheet of paper.

STEP FOUR

Together with your cartoon helper, select and draw a gift to the monsters and nightmares. This gift will turn them into what you want them to be. What would be the most powerful gift so that you can become friends? You decide, then draw it on a small sheet of paper.

(At this point, Mohammed asked if he could include his teddy bear in making the decision about the gift, and was told he could. He took the picture he drew of Bugs Bunny and his teddy bear off to a corner for a conference. About five minutes later, he returned, ready to draw an "awesome remote-control car.")

STEP FIVE

Have your cartoon helper (and your teddy bear) present this gift to the monsters and nightmares.

STEP SIX

Now draw on a smaller piece of paper how the monsters and the nightmares have changed into friends.

STEP SEVEN

Talk about this new ending to your story with the help of your cartoon friend. Doing this will help you become strong in your mind.

Hug time

AFTERWARDS

Beginning that same evening, Mohammed started sleeping through the night. He did get frightened occasionally by nightmares, but the times were much shorter and more spaced out. Even the nightmares were less intense, which allowed him to resume sleep soon after some quick comforting. It improved Dad's disposition, too, not to have his sleep interrupted on a nightly basis.

SITUATION
A child is going on a vacation away from his parents.

Two months after nine-year-old Robert had come to live with them, his two new mothers, Alix and Miriam, had taken him to visit Alix's parents in Tennessee. They spent a lot of time on the plane discussing travel, what a person needs to do and what not to do on a plane, and what to do if an emergency arises. Alix's parents said that they hoped that Robert would visit them during his February vacation even though Alix and Miriam would be working and could not accompany him. Robert was looking forward to the plane ride, but he was afraid to leave home. He wondered if his mothers might not be there when he got back. Alix had been very sick with the flu that winter, and Robert had worried that she would die and about what would happen to him. A parent's illness undoubtedly is scarier when life has been unstable, and so a ceremony was needed to put things in their proper perspective and to offer Robert reassurance when mere words would probably not be enough. Words said in a ceremony are often heard and experienced differently.

"GOING ON VACATION"

ROBERT:	This Saturday, I start February vacation for one week. I am going to visit Nanna and Grampy for the week.
MOMMY:	Unhappily, we cannot go with you because we must work. It is not our vacation time.
ROBERT:	I will miss you, but I will have a good time.
MAMA:	We will miss you, too, and we hope that you have a very good time. We want to make some promises to you and we want you to make some to us.
ROBERT:	Okay.
MOMMY:	I promise to try to stay well while you are gone. If the flu comes back, Miriam will help me, but I feel good and hope to stay that way.
MAMA:	And I promise to try to stay well while you are gone. If the flu finds me and I get sick, Alix will help me, but I feel good and hope to stay that way.
ROBERT:	I will try to stay healthy. I have been sneezing and coughing and I might get a cold. If I get a cold, Nanna and Grampy will take care of me just like they took care of Mommy when she was little. But I feel good and hope to stay healthy.
MOMMY AND MAMA:	We promise to feed your fish twice a day and to turn their light on and off.
ROBERT:	I promise to keep you in my prayers every night.
MOMMY:	I promise to keep you in my prayers every night.
MAMA:	I promise to keep you in my prayers every night.
MOMMY:	When you come back on the airplane, we will meet you at the airport.

MAMA:	We will meet you at the airport with a big smile and a big hug.
ROBERT:	And I promise to meet you with a smile and hug.
MAMA:	Sometimes when people are separated for a short time, they miss each other, but sometimes the break helps them love each other even more.
MOMMY:	Maybe we will all love each other even more when we see you again.
ROBERT:	Maybe I will love you even more, too.
MOMMY:	So we will remember our promises to each other.
ROBERT:	And we will keep our promises to each other.
EVERYONE:	And our family love will grow and grow.

Hug time

AFTERWARDS

Words mean very little to adoptees, especially older ones. They have been told by others that a move was permanent when it was temporary. Some of them had never been exposed to a sense of going and returning that a "vacation" implies. It was very important to Robert that even though he knew his mothers loved him, he also knew that he was coming back to them. The ceremony was able to calm Robert in a way that no discussion had been able to up to that point. Robert went off to enjoy his vacation with minimum trepidation and a lot of excitement.

SITUATION

Birth parents do not show up for a scheduled visit with their child.

Sheldon and Marta were foster parents to seven-year-old Olivia. When Olivia had been with them for six months, her social worker arranged for a visit with her biological mother. The biological mother had been in a rehab program for drug addicts and had been making steady progress. Sheldon and Marta didn't tell Olivia about the planned visit until the night before in order to lessen her waiting time and anxiety. They took Olivia to the social worker's office, only to find that the biological mother had not yet arrived. After waiting for 45 minutes and trying to keep Olivia amused, they finally agreed to take her home and to focus on her disappointment. Olivia was quiet and uncommunicative. Sheldon and Marta decided to try something physical and to create a ceremony around it.

"THIS IS HOW I FEEL RIGHT NOW"*

Sheldon and Marta explained that Olivia probably had a lot of feelings right now, and that all of her feelings were okay. They just wanted to help her express them in safe ways.

They put a large cushion on the floor to Olivia's left and a pile of cushions on her right. They explained that the one large cushion represented the parts of Olivia's first mother that Olivia loves no matter what. The pile of cushions represented all her other feelings piled on top of one another.

When Olivia thought of parts of her mother that she loves, she was to hug the first pillow and say how she felt. When she felt disappointment or anger or sadness, she was to hit, pound, or kick the pile of pillows. They told her that she must be careful not to hurt herself in any way. Sheldon would help her stay safe. When she hit or punched, she was to say words that would go with how she was feeling. Marta would pretend that she was the voice of the first mother and make sounds that would go with the force of the blow Olivia was delivering. Marta needed to say that she was only playing the voice of the first mother and that she would not herself feel hurt in any way (it was also important that she not appear to be hurt).

Olivia was told to begin. A wave of guilt must have hit her because she immediately went over to the single cushion and assured her first mother that she loved her. Then she went to the larger pile and, on her knees, began punching the pillows—slowly and softly at first, and then more forcefully. Sheldon reminded her to vocalize when she did anything. Marta reacted vocally to every punch, blow, and kick.

Olivia started out by saying that she was disappointed. Then she expressed her anger. And last, she dealt with her sadness. Periodically, she would move over to the cushion representing the parts of her mother she loved. Once she was able to say how she was feeling, she started to giggle while punching the pillows. Sheldon said she seemed to be feeling better. She repeated that she just wanted to punch pillows a few more times, after which she laughed for about 90 seconds.

She was reminded that the pillows were not her first mother, but

---

*This ceremony was based on the work of Albert Pesso and Diane Boyden Pesso who created the Pesso/Boyden Psychomotor System. (See Pesso & Crandell [1991].)

represented parts of her mother. They told her she could do this any time she needed to and that they would be delighted to help her.

Note: Marta made the sounds because the person was a woman. Had it been a man, Sheldon would have stepped in to make the sounds. Single parents should not be constrained by the sounds and just do the best they can in reacting.

AFTERWARDS

Sheldon and Marta reported that Olivia brightened up a lot. She loved using the pillows and would ask her parents if they would help her punch pillows for various reasons after that first time.

SITUATION
Making safety clear for a first-time foster child.

Spring, 11 years old, had been living with her biological father since her mother died two years previously. The father drank heavily and had been abusing his daughter sexually. Spring became known to the Department of Social Services through a report from her favorite teacher, who wanted to help her. Spring did not want to live with her father, but she also did not trust anyone else. Connie, the social worker, said that sexual boundaries in the home of the foster parents, Donald and Rosalie, should be clear from the beginning.

Special Note: Some people might find the language and approach in this ceremony shocking. At a conference sponsored by Project Impact (now known as Special Adoption Family Services) in Boston, a social worker from Texas shared her approach to introducing foster children who had been sexually abused to a new family where they would be safe. Her approach cut down on false accusations by angry or confused foster children against foster parents. Her main idea has been incorporated into this ceremony.

"YOU ARE SAFE HERE"

CONNIE: The purpose of this ceremony is to set up some
            clear ground rules for this home.

ROSALIE:	We know that your father was being sexual with you in ways that a father is not supposed to be with his daughter.
DONALD:	We want you to know that no matter what you do or say, we will not be sexual with you.
ROSALIE:	I have sex with Donald and no one else.
DONALD:	I have sex with Rosalie and no one else.
ROSALIE:	It is not your fault that your father had sex with you.
DONALD:	While you may be mad at your father for what he did sexually to you, you may still love him for other reasons.
ROSALIE:	We are here to help you in any way we can and in any way you will let us.
DONALD:	We are not here to say bad things about your father.
ROSALIE:	We know how to hold and hug children without being sexual. We will help you learn this, too.
DONALD:	And we know how to set limits even if you are sexual with us.
SPRING:	What if I get worried about my father or about what might happen to me?
CONNIE:	I will stop by and you can ask me any questions. You can talk to Rosalie and Donald. They can call me if you have any questions or concerns that they cannot address.
SPRING:	I don't want other kids to know why I left or why I'm here.
ROSALIE:	Kids will not know anything you do not tell them. You might think about saying that your father is having some problems right now and cannot take care of you, so you are staying here.
SPRING:	What if I do not like it here?
DONALD:	There will be times when we expect you to do things that you don't want to do, like make your bed, and you will want to leave. We will have good moments and bad moments and we will work them out together. If we need help, we will ask Connie to help us.

SPRING:	What if I wake up in the middle of the night with bad dreams?
ROSALIE:	We will be here to help you.
SPRING:	What if I need to talk about things?
DONALD:	We will be here to listen.
	We want you to remember that you are safe here. No one here will try to have sex with you.
ROSALIE:	This ceremony is over. We want you to know that the talking can continue outside of the ceremony. We would like to end this ceremony by shaking hands with everyone as a way of saying we will keep our promises.

AFTERWARDS

Rosalie and Donald together showed Spring around the house. They showed her their bedroom and said that if their door was closed, she should knock and wait to be invited in. They would extend the same courtesy to her as long as they knew she was all right. She said that she wanted to spend some time alone in her room, and Rosalie agreed. She told her that she would call her when it was time to go grocery shopping so they could buy some things Spring liked, too. When Donald asked Spring to come downstairs, she did so at the first request. She looked guarded for the first week but then started to relax and talk.

NONVERBAL ALTERNATIVES

Any situation that has elements of leaving home, having a good time, and coming home later can demonstrate a vacation. If the child is going and needs to be sure that the parents will be home when he or she returns, that must be part of the scenario. Parents can reassure children by waving goodbye while smiling and saying: "Have a great time and we'll be here waiting for you when you come home." If the parents leave, they wave goodbye and hug and kiss the children, telling them that they will be back. As part of the play, the parents might show themselves having a good time and talking about how much they love their child and can't wait to get home to see him or her. And when they do get home, they give the child a big hug, saying how much they enjoyed their vacation and how happy they were to be home. We would also recommend using props, like suitcases or duffle bags, if the kids are very small, so that packing clothes in suitcases does not upset them when they see it happening. Pretend packing could also be part of the enacted story. The parents can then reassure their children by doing some of the same things when they leave on and then return from their actual vacation. It appears like a promise made and a promise kept, which helps to build and enhance trust.

The sexual-abuse scenario is a little tricky to do nonverbally. You might purchase anatomically correct dolls, and have the dolls act out appropriate behavior. If you opt to try this, we recommend consulting with a therapist who is experienced in working with these dolls and children for advice on the best way to proceed to make a message clear without confusing, frightening, or sexually stimulating your child.

✂ 8 ✄

Ceremonies for Anniversaries

"The Day We Met"

"The First Anniversary"

"There Is Plenty of Room in a Heart"

CELEBRATING ANNIVERSARIES OF special occasions for children who have become part of a new family through adoption is a way of letting them know how much they mean to the family. It allows the newly formed family to begin to build a shared history. When the family celebrates the anniversary of the first day the adoptive parents met the child, the day the child came to live with them, or the day the adoption was legalized in court, they are creating memories together that will bring family members closer and add to the child's feelings of security. A child who feels loved and wanted will be able to cope with life's challenges more easily.

Anniversaries also bring up the feelings that accompanied the original event. These "anniversary reactions" have a way of surfacing even if there is no conscious effort to remember. So, for instance, a few days before the anniversary of the adoption legalization, the child may begin to experience uncomfortable feelings that reflect the loyalty conflict inherent in relinquishing one's birth family and becoming adopted. The child may not be aware of the reason for these feelings and so be compelled to act out in a problematic way. Any ceremony that celebrates the happy gains that the anniversary marks should also take into account the losses suffered. If the family can begin to address the painful feelings ahead of time by preparing the child to expect them, they may avert the need for difficult behavior and allow the anniversary day to be mostly celebratory.

"The Day We Met" ceremony honors this special event in the life of the newly formed family while it helps the child to verbalize his or her feelings "The First Anniversary" ceremony acknowledges the sadness of the loss of the birth family while celebrating the child's entry into the adopted family.

"Teon's First Anniversary" ceremony deals with the adoption of a second child and addresses the issue of sibling rivalry. The "There Is Plenty of Room in a Heart" ceremony helps a child overcome worries that loving the adopting parents means giving up his or her love for the birth parents.

~

SITUATION
Remembering a special day together.

George and Agnes, who had adopted nine-year-old Toni the previous year, started out by trying ceremonies with her, and she seemed really to enjoy them. The first year had been tough, but they wanted to commemorate the day they actually met her, which was a special day for them all. With a year's history behind them, they wanted to start remembering together the way families do. Toni had problems with conversations, especially those involving feelings, so they decided to do a ceremony that would call for more than her usual one-word answers. They also wanted to let Toni use more of her own words rather than rely on theirs.

"THE DAY WE MET"

MAMA:	We first met exactly one year ago. Before we met you, we saw a picture of you and heard a lot about you. We heard about things you liked and all the houses you lived in.
PAPA:	We heard that you needed a new home. We heard about very good behavior and very bad behavior. We decided before we even met you that we wanted you to be in our family.
TONI:	Before I met you, I saw a picture book that you made and I heard about you.

MAMA:	We were sure you had questions, worries, thoughts, and good and bad feelings. We wonder if you can remember these things from just before you met us.
PAPA:	Maybe you can imagine these things. If you need to close your eyes to imagine things, you may do that now.
TONI:	I knew that I would meet you after school one day. This is what I remember before I met you: My thoughts _____ My worries _____ My good feelings _____ My bad feelings _____
MAMA:	Then we met. Let's talk about that time. Who will go first? Toni, you decide.
MAMA, PAPA, AND TONI	remember together . . .
PAPA:	Now let's talk about later that night after the first time we met. What thoughts and feelings did we each have? Maybe the thoughts and feelings happened at dinner or after dinner or before we fell asleep.
TONI:	The person who will start to share is _____.
MAMA, PAPA, AND TONI	remember . . .
PAPA:	It is a year later and a lot has happened. I have grown a lot as a person and as a father. I want to tell you, Toni, one of the ways in which you have helped me. In trying to be helpful to you, I have had to try new and different things. You have helped me learn how to respond to the specialness you bring, which I like very much.
MAMA:	I also want to tell you, Toni, one of the ways in which you have helped me. I have learned that making a promise to be your mother forever was one of the best promises I ever made. Toni, what would you like to say? Please try to use at least two sentences.

TONI:	What I would like to say is:
	_____
	_____
MAMA AND PAPA:	We want to tell you some of the things we appreciate about you:
	• You are brave. You are willing to try new things. You have the courage to take the first step.
	• You are kind. You show this when you hold someone's hand when the person is frightened. You care about others.
	• You try. We often ask you to do things that you do not know how to do. You try to do your best.
MAMA:	You are unique.
PAPA:	There is no one else just like you.
MAMA:	I am glad you are my daughter.
PAPA:	I am glad you are my daughter.
MAMA AND PAPA:	We like who you are now and who you will be in the future.
MAMA:	We look forward to remembering a lot more with you.
PAPA:	And we love you bunches. Toni, please tell us three ways you feel right now.
TONI:	Three ways I feel right now are:
	_____
	_____
	_____

Hugs all around

AFTERWARDS

Toni needed a pencil. She wanted to think about her answers, then write them down, and then read them. While the process felt drawn out to her parents, Toni did not mind the pacing or the work at all. It worked out nicely for Toni. It was a process that helped her put more of her own thoughts and energy into the action—which is what they had hoped for anyway. They experienced a lot of smiling and perkiness on Toni's part that she rarely showed when they just talked.

~

SITUATION

Celebrating the first anniversary of a child's adoption.

When Catherine and Jeremiah adopted eight-year-old Claude, they already had one birth child, Kira, who was 10 years old at the time. After Claude had been in the family for a year, they decided to celebrate the anniversary of his arrival. They enlisted Kira's help in putting the ceremony together so that she was included in an empowering way. That helped both children feel special. Kira helped to choose a cake for the event. Visiting relatives were included in the ceremony as well.

"THE FIRST ANNIVERSARY"

KIRA:	This day is our first anniversary of becoming a family by law.
MOM AND DAD:	We were a family in our hearts before we became a family by law. One year ago today, we became a forever family officially.
COUSIN ALFRED:	I am your cousin forever by law and in my heart.
AUNT SYLVIA:	I am your aunt forever by law and in my heart.
UNCLE MIKE:	I am your uncle forever by law and in my heart.
CLAUDE:	Yes, we are a family forever. Alfred, you are my cousin forever; Sylvia, you are my aunt forever; and Mike, you are my uncle forever. Kira, you are my sister forever; and Mom and Dad, you are my parents forever.
MOM:	Anniversaries can be happy and sad at the same time. They are a beginning and an ending, too.
DAD:	This anniversary marks the time when we became a family and it meant this was for keeps no matter what.
CLAUDE:	It also meant that while I can see my first mom and dad, I cannot live with them anymore. So I can have lots of different feelings and they are all okay.
EVERYBODY:	That's right!

Mom and Dad:	We promise to help Claude and Kira grow in a home of love.
Kira and Claude:	We promise to accept your love and help.
Everybody:	(Each person says how he or she feels at the moment: Sylvia, Mike, Alfred, Kira, Claude, Mom, and Dad.)
Kira:	Our first anniversary ceremony is over. No one can ever separate us.
Claude:	This is for keeps!
Group hug	

AFTERWARDS

When a child is born into a family, the birthday marks that occasion. Even though these parents knew that a child can have sad feelings about no longer being with the birth parents, they did not want that to keep them from marking the day as special and important. They also wanted to remind Claude that even though he was not their child by birth, as Kira was, his place in the family was just as strong. Everyone enjoyed the ceremony and the cake afterwards. It was just enough.

SITUATION

Celebrating the first anniversary of the adoption of a second child.

Jeff, a single father, had adopted Aaron three years previously, when Aaron was nine, and then two years later, adopted Teon, who was seven. Jeff wanted each boy to have an anniversary celebration. Three months earlier, they had had a ceremony for Aaron and now were doing one for Teon. Jeff knew that in spite of Aaron's having had a ceremony of his own, he would have a problem with Teon's being given something special. It was not an issue of fairness, but of Aaron's not wanting to share his father with Teon. The year had been rocky, and Jeff decided to acknowledge the rockiness as part of the ceremony. He understood that anniversaries can be a mixed bag for the kids. Whereas they were joyful occasions for Jeff, they marked finality for the boys, who would never be reconciled with their respective birth families. The boys knew that, and although they were strongly attached to Jeff, he recognized that they still hoped for a miracle.

"TEON'S FIRST ANNIVERSARY"

TEON:	One year ago today, I was adopted.
DAD:	It is hard for me to believe that one whole year has gone by.
AARON:	A lot of changes have taken place since you came. There is a lot more sharing of my toys, my books, and our father.
DAD:	Yes, and there is more fighting.
TEON:	Yes, there are fights.
AARON:	Yes, but there are good parts, too. We can play with each other and have fun together.
DAD:	I think it would be good if we each said one thing that is hard about being in one family and one thing that is easy and good about being in one family.
EVERYONE:	(Each says what he thinks)
TEON:	I have been Teon H. Marcus legally for one year.
AARON:	I have been Aaron D. Marcus for three years.
DAD:	The Marcus family is a wonderful family. There are many aunts and uncles and cousins left for both of you to meet. It will take years for you to meet all of them. You are part of a big family that is happy to have you. And we still have a lot of learning to do as a family.
AARON:	Yes, we still have a lot of learning to do as a family. We need to learn how to solve problems better.
TEON:	We do still have a lot of learning to do as a family. We need to learn how to fight fairly and keep our word.
DAD:	We need to try to be truthful and to treat each other with respect.
AARON:	So, three months ago, we celebrated my adoption and my special day.
TEON:	Today we celebrate my adoption and my special day.
ALL:	Yes, we are a family. Forever. Aaron, Teon, and Dad.

Everyone hugs

AFTERWARDS

On that particular night the boys had a good time. They had their arms on each other's shoulders more than usual and any play was good-natured. That total happiness was not destined to last forever, but for one night, it was a nice break.

~

SITUATION

Anniversary ceremony at a time when a child has become reticent about discussing her birth family.

Toby, 14 years old, had been adopted by Belinda six years earlier, Toby had had regular supervised visits with her birth mother until the birth mother moved to another state, making visiting much more difficult. Although the birth mother was absent physically, Belinda recognized that she was with them constantly. At an adoption seminar, she watched a training tape of an interview with a child getting ready to see his birth mother for the first time in 10 years. In the video, one of the things the child told the interviewer was that whenever he started to feel a lot of love in his heart for his adoptive mother, he became afraid that he would lose his love for his birth mother. This tension caused him to lash out at his adoptive mother. Belinda wanted to address the possibility that Toby might feel similar tension, even though she had never admitted it. Belinda had been doing ceremonies annually with Toby, and decided to construct one to fit this situation.

"THERE IS PLENTY OF ROOM IN A HEART"

MOMMY:	This is the sixth anniversary of our being a family.
TOBY:	Yes, I was adopted six years ago.
MOMMY:	I know that today can feel confusing to you.
TOBY:	Yes, I feel happy to be adopted and sad not to be with my first mom.
MOMMY:	I understand that. I also know that as a mother can have plenty of room in her heart for more than one child, a child can have room in her heart for more than one mother.

TOBY: Sometimes that gets confusing. I feel that if I love my first mom, that I am not being loyal to you, and if I love you, I might run out of love for my first mom.

MOMMY: The amazing thing about a heart is that it never runs out of room for love. It is like a brain—there is plenty of room for knowledge in a brain, and in a heart there is plenty of room for love.

TOBY: So I can love my first mom and you—I do not have to pick one or the other.

MOMMY: Yes, that is true. As part of this ceremony, we are each going to take a piece of paper and draw the people we love in our hearts. In a picture, remember we cannot show depth and that each of our hearts is deep enough to hold lots and lots of love. (Pause to draw pictures.)

MOMMY: Now our pictures are completed. And there is a lot for us to think about. I feel happy that you are my daughter.

TOBY: I feel_____that I am your daughter.

MOMMY: And I respect and honor your love for your first mom forever.

TOBY: And I can love two moms—I do not have to pick one.

MOMMY: That's right. So happy anniversary!

TOBY: Happy anniversary.

Hug

AFTERWARDS

Toby seemed a little embarrassed at the point where each of them was to draw a heart and put names in it. She waited for her mother to start. They helped each other think of people, and her mother encouraged copying each other so that each could enrich what the other was doing. Toby seemed to enjoy the task once she got started. After the ceremony was over, they gave each other a hug. Toby was much more cheerful for several weeks after. She held onto the picture she had drawn for about six months, when Belinda saw it in the trash and asked about it. Toby told her that she did not need the picture anymore—she had it inside of her.

NONVERBAL ALTERNATIVES: ANNIVERSARIES

A good way to celebrate anniversaries is to look at pictures—snapshots, slides, home videos. As you develop history with your child, you can reminisce together. You might draw pictures together of what you remember or were feeling when you first met and how things are different now.

You can make anniversary cards or pictures for each other, or with each other, to mark the occasion. Don't forget that a child can feel both sad and happy on an anniversary. If sad feelings are expressed by your children, it is a reflection that they feel comfortable with you; it's not unhappiness with you as a parent. Anniversaries are also a reminder of their past before they came to live with you. Cheri goes out to dinner with each boy on the anniversary of his adoption. She also plans a special ceremony for each son, usually to take place the same night. The special time has become a ceremony in and of itself. Cheri and her children spend some time talking about any milestones; for example, at one point, each child had lived with her longer than he had lived with everyone else combined. That was a significant milestone!

You can start a notebook of anniversary thoughts and ideas and add to it each year. Some of the entries might be drawings or ideas or stories—even stories dictated by the child for the parent to write down. Include a few favorite photographs. If you went on a family vacation, say where. You can write down a child's height and weight and compare them year after year. You can write: "One thing I remember especially this year is the day you lost your first tooth or the day I got my first dog . . ." It's like a "baby book" updated yearly instead of month by month. Don't make it too elaborate or you'll lose interest in doing it.

❧ 9 ❧

Ceremonies for Remembering

"Remembering When We Met"

"The Candle Ceremony"

A CHILD ADOPTED after being separated from a biological family and spending time with one or more foster families has very confused memories or, what is more likely, he or she has chosen to deny the past. The past may signify physical pain as the result of abuse or neglect or the pain of losing those who no longer are a part of the child's life. It may be easier to forget the past than to face the feelings that arise when remembering.

Also, many children who have spent their early years in a dysfunctional family, or as one of several foster children, will have few pictures or keepsakes. Social workers who prepare these children for adoption often compile "Life Books" to help a child understand his or her past. Because few or no pictures are available, magazine illustrations are used to represent the child at different ages.

Parents who adopt an older child miss important pieces of the child's life. They, too, feel the lack of pictures and information about the child's development. It becomes a matter of great importance for both the parents and the child to develop a shared history and to celebrate this new and wonderful phenomenon by making time to remember.

Remembering ceremonies can provide a context for sharing memories of their life together as a family. The "Remembering When We Met" ceremony is an example of how to construct a remembering ceremony that encourages the child to remember not only what happened, but also his or her feelings at the time. "The Candle Ceremony" provides a way of remembering back to a child's birth and paying tribute to the important people in the child's life before he or she became part of your family.

⌒

SITUATION
Remembering when an adopted son and his new mother met.

On the anniversary of the day they actually met for the first time, Debra and her eight-year-old son, Joseph, did a ceremony. It was a way of remembering. It was a way of creating a family history.

"REMEMBERING WHEN WE MET"

MOM: One year ago, we met. Before I met you, I saw a picture of you and heard a lot about you. I heard about things you liked. I heard about all the houses you lived in. I heard about very good behavior and very bad behavior. I decided even before I met you that I wanted you to be my family.

JOSEPH: Before I met you, I saw a big picture book that you made and I heard about you. I had questions, worries, thoughts, and good and bad feelings.

MOM: I wonder if you can remember your questions or worries or feelings just before you met me. If you cannot remember, maybe you can imagine these things. If you need to close your eyes to imagine things, you may.

JOSEPH: I do remember seeing the picture book and hearing about you. I knew I would meet you the next day after school. This is what I remember:

My worries _____

My good feelings _____

My bad feelings _____

My questions _____

MOM:	Then we met the next day. Let's talk about that time. Who will start, you or I? (Joseph and Mom remember together.)
JOSEPH:	Now, let's talk about later that night. What thoughts or feelings did we each have? You go first. (Mom starts, followed by Joseph.)
MOM:	It is a year later and a lot has happened. One of my favorite moments was the day we were in the yard and I asked you to go into the house and take off your shoes and come back out. Then I turned the hose on you. You got it away from me and turned it on me. We were both very wet. We had a good laugh. I smile when I think about that. Do you remember that?
JOSEPH:	One thing I remember is _____
MOM:	I remember the day you got so mad at school that you brought home a piece of the wall of the time-out room.
JOSEPH:	One thing I remember about school is _____
MOM:	I look forward to watching you grow and helping you to be the best person you can be. I look forward to making more memories.
JOSEPH:	I look forward to more silly moments and exciting adventures.
MOM:	I am glad you are my son. I like who you are today and who you will be in the future. And I love you bunches.
JOSEPH:	How I feel right now is _____
MOM:	Here's to more memories!
Hug	

AFTERWARDS

Joseph had some difficulty filling in the blanks and needed some help from his mother. For example, when he was asked what his worries were, he shrugged his shoulders. His mother asked him if he was worried that this might not work out. She got a nod and proceeded to help coax other answers out of him, using positive thoughts and some negative thoughts—and making sure that all the answers were acceptable. The next time they did some remembering together, Joseph was able to participate fully without being coaxed.

⌐⌐

SITUATION
Helping a child to address the loss of her birth parents.

Victoria and Abigail, who had been in a committed relationship for 13 years, had adopted 12-year-old Verbeena seven months earlier. Verbeena had mentioned on occasion that she still remembered her old mom and dad. Her new parents wanted to make sure that she understood that she could remember and love them for her whole life. It was suggested that Claudia Jewett Jarratt's (1982) "Candle Ceremony" might be useful here, not just to address loss, but also to remember. Abigail and Victoria had consistently tried to reassure Verbeena, but agreed that a special ceremony might help.

Preparation: The parents bought two boxes of Hanukkah candles, as these were the right size (larger than a birthday candle, but smaller than most other candles) and came in assorted colors. They also provided a box of matches, some paper, a pencil, and a piece of wood. Prior to the ceremony, they heated the bottom of a candle and placed it on the wood. It seemed to stick so they decided to use the wood rather than candleholders. They agreed ahead of time as to which of them would supervise the candle lighting and which would write down names. They opted to wait to put the candles on the board so that Verbeena could choose the color of candle she wanted to represent each person she named. As a safety measure, they held the ceremony on the kitchen floor.

"THE CANDLE CEREMONY"	

MOTHER:	When you were born, you had the gift to give love and get love. This gift is like a light. It makes you feel warm and happy. (Abigail picks out a candle to represent Verbeena, puts it on the board, and lights it.)
VERBEENA:	Since the day I was born, I have known and loved many people. This ceremony is to remember some of them.
MAMA:	Your first mom and dad had some grown-up troubles. They never learned how to take care of a little

girl. It was decided that you would need to live some-
where else, even though their love for you still
burned and your love for them was bright.

(Verbeena chooses two candles and Abigail helps by attaching them to the
board while Victoria keeps the chart of which candles represent which people. Then Verbeena lights the candles.)

MOTHER: Who were some of the other people you knew and
loved before you came to live here?

(Verbeena names other people she can remember and lights a candle for
each one.)

MAMA: Now that you live with us and we have a family,
you have other people who love you and whom
you love. Some of them are my mother and father,
and my mother's father. There are Cousin Penny,
Aunt Wendy, Uncle Zack, and others. Can you
name any other?

VERBEENA: (Names another)

MOTHER: And us. As a family, we each have one more person to love and one more person who loves us. An
important thing to remember is that the light of love
you feel for your old mom will not go out.

VERBEENA: Loving is not like soup that you serve until it is all
gone. You can love many people. I do not have to
take the love I feel for my old mom away to love
my new mom.

MAMA: I can see, Verbeena, that you understand about loving. I don't think you need the candles any more to
help you. (Lights a candle and holds it.) This candle
represents me, but it is not really me. I will not stop
loving you if we put it out. Are you ready to help
me blow it out?

VERBEENA: Yes. (Mama and Verbeena blow it out.)

VERBEENA: (repeats the phrase for each candle)
This candle is not really _____. _____ will
not stop loving me if I blow it out. Are you ready to
help me blow it out? (Both parents say Yes and
help Verbeena blow out one candle at a time.)

MOTHER: Our candle ceremony is over and loving continues.

MAMA: Our candle ceremony is over and loving continues.

VERBEENA: Our candle ceremony is over and loving continues.

Group hug

AFTERWARDS

Verbeena used a lot of candles. One person kept a written list of who was represented by each candle in case anyone forgot (that did happen). Verbeena seemed to find the ceremony meaningful and asked to do it twice more during the year. These were not on significant dates, but when she was feeling especially sad.

NONVERBAL ALTERNATIVES: REMEMBERING

An anniversary notebook can be a wonderful vehicle for remembering.

Children love to hear stories about themselves when they were younger. They especially love to hear stories about how all of you came to be a family. Telling those stories can be a ceremoney, too.

If "The Candle Ceremony" is too complicated, you might tie a small piece of ribbon onto a long piece of ribbon to represent all the people in your child's life who took care of him or her at one point or another. Even if you can't remember or don't know all the names of the people and families, a ribbon can be, for example, a place-holder for the family between the Smith and the Black families.

∂ 10 ∾

Spontaneous Ceremonies

OUR GIFT FOR play and pretending as a child seems to get lost as we become adults. Having children allows us to recapture this gift, if we can stay open to it. A spontaneous ceremony happens when a child does something to create it. In fact, in most cases, the child directs and leads the event.

The following are examples of four spontaneous ceremonies that began for different reasons and in different ways.

One of Cheri's sons needed safe and acceptable ways to express his anger. Cheri had found Pesso/Boyden System Psychomotor Therapy (developed by Albert Pesso and Diane Boyden Pesso; see Pesso & Crandell [1991]) to be self-affirming while taking advantage of movement and sound. She used this to help her son put together a pounding-pillows event that he initiated and directed. The only guideline was that he should not hurt himself or others. Her son would stack up several large pillows. He would then get a favorite stuffed animal, which he would put on one side of the stack of pillows. The stuffed animal represented the part of the person that he loved even though at the moment he was very angry at that person. If, at any time during pounding the pillows, he felt guilty, he was to stop and hug the loved aspect of the person at whom he was angry (represented by the stuffed animal), and then proceed to pound the pillows again. When pounding pillows, he was encouraged to make sounds, and even to say the words for how he felt. His mother would make sounds comparable to his anger intensity so that he got some reaction, even though she made sure that she never looked hurt. She would make the sounds in reaction as his blows hit the pillows. If he tapped the pillows, she would make a small sound. If he bashed the pillows, she would make a large sound. It was not unusual for anger to turn into laughter at some point during the process. Sometimes, if he could not find his voice, she would try to guess what the words might be for him, using the intensity of her voice to match the intensity of the hit. Her son could pound pillows without her, but it was not as satisfying without the vocal reaction.

One day, when Cheri's helper called to tell her that the helper and Cheri's son had had a terrible afternoon and tensions were running high, Cheri promised that when she got home, they would have a family council meeting—although she had no idea of what a family council meeting would be like. What she did was to ask everyone to sit on big pillows in the living room, explaining that a family council meeting had several guidelines: Everyone got to say what he or she needed to say about what had happened and how he or she felt. The others were to listen carefully, and then would have all the time they needed to respond. They would go back and forth until they figured out what had happened and how to prevent it from happening again. Cheri told her son that he could begin. The adults followed his lead until all the conversation necessary had taken place and a plan was put in place for next time. Her son then said that for the council to be over, he needed a group hug. He requested a family council meeting one other time over the years, stating the guidelines in his own words and managing the process completely.

Another spontaneous ceremony was inspired by a son's two-hour temper tantrum, after which a lot of hurt feelings came pouring out. They talked about his having had a lousy beginning and how he needed to mourn for his unhappy childhood. Cheri explained that in Judaism, when people lose a person through death, they sit shiva for one week, during which they remember the person who died and let others take care of them. Cheri said that maybe he needed to sit shiva for the part of his childhood that he had lost and could never have back again. She then planned a day, most of which would be devoted to her taking care of her son while he mourned. They wrote on index cards the names of people whom her son would never see again because they had died, of those whom he might see again, and of the new people in his life, and then placed the cards on different parts of a large sheet of paper. Cheri wanted him to see that with endings there are also beginnings and that he had gained a lot. She then asked him to take an index card and do something for the childhood he lost that was not happy, that he would never have back. He drew a picture of a man with an ax chopping down a small tree piece by piece. They spent the day talking, crying, laughing, and playing. When the day was over, Cheri said it was time to move forward together, remembering and affirming what had come before and knowing that there would be new experiences ahead.

This last example is Cheri's favorite. One night her son asked how people got started. She asked him if he wanted to know how babies were born and he said No, that his question was really how people got started. Cheri briefly described two options: creation and evolution. He said he liked the creation story and then said that while they were on the subject, could they also discuss how babies come to be. After a brief explanation, which he paraphrased as they went along, he said, "Let's do it." Cheri was not sure how he wanted to do the story of birth, but waited for his lead. He said that he would crawl inside his covers down to the end of his bed. He would pretend that he was in a birth canal and would come out when he was born. After coming out as different types of babies, he said that the next would take a long time. When he came out, she would need to help him gently. He crawled down under his covers and began struggling and making noises as if he were genuinely struggling. After about eight minutes, he emerged slowly, head first, from his covers, and Cheri eased him out gently as instructed. He started to cry and sound like a newborn. Cheri just held him. She then said that when mothers have their babies, they support them completely. So they rearranged themselves and she held him as he lay in her lap, supporting his entire weight. She started to sing softly, and he told her she was singing the wrong song. He asked her to sing "Happy Birthday." He had rebirthed himself with his new mother.

These examples were of times when talking alone would not have worked. Cheri was not exactly sure what to do in these cases. Perhaps it was frustration, or she was trying to break a pattern that was not working. There are no rules, only opportunities.

∝ 11 ∾

Magic Ceremonies

Rational thinking and logic are often lost on children when they are afraid, and so magic might prove useful in this case.

Cheri's first venture into magic came during the first thunderstorm when her son asked to sleep with her. She initially tried the bowling analogy, that the angels were bowling and getting strikes. When her son kept insisting that he sleep with her, she told him that they needed to help him feel safe in his bed. She remembered a storyteller on television telling children how to deal with fear. She decided to take the idea and relate it to thunder and lightning. She told her son that if he took his left shoe and pointed it to the left and then took his right shoe and pointed it to the right, and then made sure that the heels were touching, he would be safe. It worked with some variations her son created. For example, if the storm were especially intense, he would ask for a pair of his mom's shoes, assuming that bigger shoes would offer more protection. If he needed to go to the bathroom, he would carry the shoes with him and place them outside the door.

Her other son expressed a serious fear one night. He said he thought that a woman in black was hiding in his closet. He even said that he knew she was not real. Cheri turned on the light and together they examined the closet. He could see that no one was there. However, he explained that she was hiding and would reappear once his mother left the room whether or not the lights were on. Cheri decided that magic was needed here. She positioned her son's large teddy bear near the bed and facing the closet. She then told her son that the teddy bear would protect him. When he protested that it was not real, she reminded him that he said that the woman in black was not real either, so what better way to protect against something not real but with something else not real. Her son seemed relieved, agreed with her, and went to sleep. He would, on his own, position the large teddy bear facing the closet until the fear had dissipated, a few days later.

Both of Cheri's sons were afraid to go down into the basement—a dry, well-lighted space that had areas in which they could play safely—because there were monsters there. Cheri was not successful in helping them work out this fear, until she saw a scene in "The Parent Trap," a Disney movie, in which children teased an adult unused to camping about how she needed to beat two sticks together to keep wild animals away. The adult believed them and Cheri decided, "That's it." She bought two dowels that were the same width and length and had them cut in half. She then bought some blue paper, which was self-adhering on one side, and covered the sticks. When her children came home, she told them that she had found the secret to managing the monsters in the basement. She showed them the "monster sticks," explaining that when they were tapped together, they would scare the monsters away and the boys could play safely. There was one catch. If they used the monster sticks for any other purpose, such as like swords or weapons (especially on each other), the magic would go out of the sticks. The boys were excited and wanted to try them, even though it was dark out—as that would be a tougher test. They asked their mother to stay upstairs while they went into the basement. From their first-floor apartment, Cheri could hear them clicking the sticks together. After a while, they came running up, joyful and excited, stating that the monster sticks really worked. Several years later, she was walking down to the basement when she heard her younger son telling their new four-year-old neighbor that he had nothing to worry about and that he could use the monster sticks, too.

Both boys were complaining of problems with their homework. Cheri believed that the work was not too difficult, but that their confidence level was low. Lynda, who helped Cheri with the boys during the week, came up with an idea that they used with success for one school year. They got a non-name-brand vitamin that would be safe for children and a large, empty pill container. On a label, they typed, "Smart Pills for Eric and Chris." Cheri explained to the boys that these pills were very hard to obtain and needed to be kept a secret or everyone would want them. If each boy took one, and only one, each day, he would be able to concentrate and get his homework done faster and easier. In addition, Cheri had obtained "lucky pencils" for the kids to use to do their homework. The combination of the two aided homework and the children were delighted. The pencils, purchased through a mail order catalog, had "Eric's lucky pencils" and "Chris' lucky pencils" printed on them and on the box that held them.

Another child who was going through a very fearful time was afraid of baths, saying that anything in the tub could hurt her. Cheri recommended that the mother buy food coloring and prepare a bath with her daughter's favorite color. She made her daughter a red bath one night, and the fear disappeared. The food coloring (which does not stay in the tub or on the child) either distracted her or camouflaged the particles in the water enough that the bath was a huge success.

As Cheri's children have grown older, neither has ever challenged her on the magic she used. It worked in the moment and helped them face fears that even they knew made no sense, but that to them were very real.

◄ 12 ►

Ceremonies for Special Situations

INTERNATIONAL ADOPTIONS

MORE FAMILIES ARE becoming multicultural. As telecommunications bring people from all parts of the world close together and ease of airplane travel allows for greater face-to-face contact, we are becoming more familiar and comfortable with differences. Marriage between partners of different cultures and religions is more common and the children of these unions enjoy the benefits of their varied heritages.

Adoption, too, has gone beyond the borders of the United States, and Americans are adopting children from Asian, Eastern European, South American, and Spanish cultures. Parents adopting children from other countries are urged to familiarize themselves with the traditions, clothing, food, and history of their child's homeland. Such organizations as the Open Door Society of Massachusetts and SPACE (Single Parents for Adopted Children Everywhere) provide a way for parents and children to meet with other families with adopted children from the same country. Those parents who go to a child's country to pick up that child have the opportunity to take pictures and meet people there, which will enliven and inform their discussion when the child grows older and becomes curious about his or her roots. A child's pride in his or her cultural heritage can only help to enhance self-esteem.

It is a good idea to incorporate the ceremonial traditions of your child's country of birth into the life of your family. In cases where the other culture celebrates the same holidays that you do, the customs can be added to your own celebrations. For instance, many countries celebrate Christmas, but each has its own particular traditions, foods, decorations, and religious rituals. Adding aspects of the holiday traditions of your child's native country can give new meaning to the celebration of your own holidays.

For rituals that are unique to your child's country of birth, you may want to work with other parents of children from the same country to research, plan, and celebrate these special occasions.

CHILDREN FROM RACES OTHER THAN YOUR OWN, OR OF MIXED RACE

African-American, Native-American, Asian-American and Latino children, as well as children of mixed parentage, present a different dilemma in adoption. These three groups are an integral part of American life, and yet have distinct cultural heritages. And in view of the racism that permeates our society, they place great emphasis on generational continuity and the importance of teaching their children how to survive in a racist world.

Current adoption practice supports the placement of children with families much like the families into which they were born, those of a similar race and culture. But a good adoption involves finding an adoptive family that both will educate the child about his or her racial and cultural background, and, equally important, provide the child with a diverse community in which to grow up.

INFANTS

There are many traditions that surround the entry of a new child into the family, whether by birth or adoption—giving baby showers, passing out cigars, sending birth announcements, plus religious rituals, such as baptism, christening, circumcision, and naming. (For example, see "Thanksgiving for the Birth or Adoption of a Child," *Episcopal Book of Common Prayer*.) These ceremonies are meant more for the parents than they are for the child. The parents are anxious to share their happiness with their extended family, friends, and co-workers, and to bask in the warmth of their reciprocal support. The child benefits in later years when shown pictures and mementos of these events, and comes to understand the importance of his or her entry into the family.

Many families choose to augment the traditional forms of celebration with more personalized ceremonies. They may add words to the basic ritual to reflect their own thoughts and feelings, or they may create completely new ceremonies with readings, songs, and poetry that are meaningful to them.

TEENAGERS

The only adoptees for whom ceremonies might not be easy to do are those adopted as teenagers. Given the distrust, suspiciousness of new things, and efforts to be "cool" that govern adolescent life, parents may find it impossible to get their child to even consider participating. But that doesn't mean that you shouldn't try. The key may be to work closely with your teenage child in planning the ceremony so that he or she can feel part of the process. The teenager may be more interested if he or she has some control.

And if you start doing ceremonies when your child is younger, as a teenager, he or she is more likely to consider the ceremonies as part of family life and to welcome them.

❧ 13 ❧

Barriers to Conducting Ceremonies

Y OU NOW KNOW why, and how, ceremonies can be helpful in orienting your adoptive child to his or her new life, but you may find that writing and enacting them is not that easy. The following addresses some of the barriers that may stand in the way of using and benefiting from the ceremonies that have been described.

One possible barrier relates to how comfortable adoptive parents may be in dealing with their child's feelings about his or her birth parents. When you have adopted a child old enough to have known and have memories of the birth parents, it often seems as though the birth parents have moved in along with the child. A child's connection to his or her birth parents is a powerful one, and no amount of abuse or neglect on their part can sever the child's ties to them. While adoptive parents may feel outrage at the suffering a child has endured because of the birth parents' emotional, mental, or physical problems, the child would rather see himself or herself as the cause of those problems than think badly of a parent.

It may not be easy to write a ceremony when you, as the adoptive parent, not only have to include comments about the birth parents, but also make sure that you highlight their best qualities. You will need to extend the compassion you feel for your child to his or her parents. You can approach this difficult task by honestly acknowledging that most parents do not wish to harm their children deliberately. Rather, in their own early life experiences, their needs were not met and, as adults, they did not have the inner resources to meet their children's needs. In seeking ways to get their needs met, they turned to inappropriate partners, to drugs, and/or to alcohol. As a result, their children suffered and outsiders were called upon to care for them. Many birth parents are overwhelmed by guilt and shame that prevent them from maintaining contact with their children. You will find that as you keep your promises to your children and follow through in providing for them, they will see the differences between you and their birth parents without your having to point them out. It is in your and your child's best interests to express empathy with the birth parents, and, in your ceremonies, to acknowledge that they undoubtedly wished to be good parents, but were unable to carry it out.

Most children, and all older children, placed for adoption have spent some time in foster care. Such stays range from several weeks to several years, and many older children have been in more than one foster home. For children without biological family connections, foster parents are the only family they know, and leaving them to enter an adoptive home can stir up conflicting feelings.

It's not always easy for adoptive parents to cope with the competition of a foster family, especially when your child tells you how much better the foster parents did something or other. But it is important to honor a child's commitment to the foster parents, as it reflects his or her ability to connect, and is a clue as to how he or she will feel about you in the future.

It might be better for your child if you were to "adopt" some of the rituals and ceremonies that were celebrated in the foster home as a way of showing that you accept his or her past. Over time, these rituals can be replaced by the ones you create as a family, or may continue as additions to your own.

As you create ceremonies to deal with problems that are affecting your child and family life, you may also find yourself faced with the dilemma of whether to avoid an issue in the hope that it will go away or to bring it up and deal with painful feelings. Your extended-family members and close friends may recommend against dealing with this issue; you, your spouse, and other children in the family may also have differing opinions. Unfortunately, no problem ever really disappears just because it's not talked about. If you push something away here, it bubbles up there, and often in a form so different that you may not recognize it. The best course is to bite the bullet and address difficult issues in the ceremony form. By assigning each person in your family a part in the ceremony, you can keep the child with the problem from feeling alone with his or her pain. Performing the ceremony can draw you all closer.

When writing the ceremony, parents may wonder whether they might not be putting words into other people's mouths that don't really express how they feel. These fears of making mistakes can make it difficult to get started. The answer is to take the plunge with the understanding that anyone can change his or her part if it doesn't feel right. It may then be a short step to finding the right words.

✑ 14 ✑

Troubleshooting Guide

Twenty Questions—and Answers

1. **Q:** I started to do a ceremony with my daughter and found myself feeling impatient with her slow reading. What should I have done?

   A: You probably did not remember that you need to be rested and ready for doing a ceremony. If it happens again, inwardly acknowledge your impatience and try to shift your attention to your child's needs and the ceremony. And try to remember that the next time you have had a bad day or are overtired or feeling impatient, you can postpone the ceremony.

2. **Q:** My spouse and I developed a wonderful ceremony. We worked very hard and were very excited and anxious to try it. Our son went through the motions, but seemed to be disinterested. What went wrong?

   A: You may have created a ceremony to meet your needs and not those of your child. If not, perhaps the task or language was beyond your son's capability. When you sense his disinterest, you might also ask your son whether he wants to continue or would like to postpone the ceremony to another time. If you keep the ceremony short and focused on only one issue, this is less likely to happen.

3. **Q:** After I started a ceremony with my children, first the telephone rang and then the doorbell. It was very distracting. How can I handle that better in the future?

A: Try to remember to take the telephone and the fax phone off the hook next time. Even an answering machine picking up calls may not be a solution if the ringing of the phone distracts your child. If you need to answer the door, just say something like, "Time out. Hold your place and I'll be right back," and either attend to the door quickly or ask someone not participating in the ceremony to do so. Return at once and sit down, ready to continue. If the child seems to have left the ceremony physically or mentally, you can say that you can do it another time. Children don't mind repetition as much as we do.

4. **Q:** My daughter refused to participate in the ceremony that we worked so hard to create. We were surprised and disappointed. Now what?

   A: Say, "Okay, we will do it when you feel ready." If she does not indicate a readiness within a reasonable time, try again to introduce it. The theme may be wrong or too threatening, or your child may be having too rough a time to go through a ceremony. Don't force it. It won't be effective and you won't enjoy it.

5. **Q:** We started a ceremony and then realized our son was too tired. What should we do next time?

   A: Stop immediately and say that you are sorry, but you did not realize how tired he was and that you can do the ceremony another time. If you have not started and your child is expecting a ceremony, I suggest you wait until he is more rested.

6. **Q:** The ceremony we designed took a turn we hadn't planned. We looked at each other and did not know what to do. My partner got it back on track. What do we do if it happens again?

   A: Go with the flow. Sometimes where a child goes is where he or she needs to go. Think of it as play and follow the child's lead. For the future, review the ceremony. Could you have misinterpreted the need and the child took it where he or she needed to go? Did you try to do too much in one ceremony and the child focussed in on only one direction? You can always say that the ceremony went in a direction that was different from how you thought it might, but you were pleased that your child did what made sense to him or her. Be gentle with yourself. Don't be too critical.

7. **Q:** My child is very shy and might be easily embarrassed. Should I still try ceremonies?

   A: Take that into account when you plan the ceremony. Go slowly and start small. Just do short ceremonies with the immediate family. Don't involve others until the child is more comfortable.

8. **Q:** My child is very defiant and probably won't agree to try a ceremony. Should I even bother?

   A: One boy who was very defiant refused to do a lot of things, but he never refused to do ceremonies. He loved them. During a ceremony, he could focus on things that he would not discuss in a conversation. He liked lighting candles before the ceremony started and getting something afterwards. Twice when he needed to say goodbye to a social worker, he initially refused to participate, but when reminded of the gift at the end, he did so willingly.

9. **Q:** Isn't giving a small gift like giving a bribe and encouraging a materialistic attitude?

   A: The tokens kids get at the end of ceremonies are small, very simple items. For example, it could be a very tiny teddy bear with the spoken message, "I love you 'beary' much." The token gift helps to anchor the messages and feelings related to the ceremony. The gifts should never be valuable monetarily. One parent gave a child a decorative fork that had been reshaped into a work of art, and told him that he was unique, like the fork. The son was not too happy with the fork initially, but whenever anyone came to the house over the next week, he would show his fork, explaining that he was unique, like the fork.

10. **Q:** My children and I were doing a ceremony and one of them started to cry quietly. I pretended I didn't notice and kept going with the ceremony. Was that the right thing to do?

    A: There is always more than one right answer to every question. Here are some options. Say: "I can see that you are very sad. Do you need a hug?" You can also say: "I can see that something made you feel very sad. Can you tell me what did?" Use the present moment. After the child calms down, ask if he or she would like to continue the ceremony or stop. If one child wants to continue and the other wants to stop, you can respect both choices. You can excuse one child and continue with the other. You could do the ceremony another night for one or both, or maybe you did enough. Tears are not a sign of failure, but of success—you may have tapped some place very important for your child and you were there to help. It doesn't get better than that.

11. **Q:** We were doing a serious ceremony with our son and he started acting silly and goofy. We raised our voices and got annoyed. We finished it, but the moment was ruined by his acting out and our yelling. Help!

    A: You may have tapped another emotion that got displayed as silly and goofy. Start by asking what is so funny or silly. Sometimes a phrase can strike one as funny quite out of context. It does not mean being disrespectful. It may mean a real but different connection. If this proves to be wrong and your child is just in a silly mood, you may want to postpone the ceremony. Don't sound angry. Just say that perhaps you picked the wrong time for the ceremony and will do it another time. Also, humor is an odd thing. There can be a lot of insight through humor. As long as people are laughing together in a way that does not make anyone uncomfortable, it might be a good addition to your ceremony.

12. **Q:** My child has trouble with matches and setting fires so I don't want to use candles to mark the moment. What do I use?

   A: Potpourri makes a nice alternative. Everyone can throw a little into a bowl of water. Or you can just say something, such as, "Now is the time for our ceremony to begin." The child can recite the name of the ceremony. At the end you can say, "Our ceremony is now over."

13. **Q:** We have two children and a particular ceremony is meant more for one than for the other. How do we handle this?

   A: If the other child can grasp the meaning of the ceremony, let him or her participate, as well. No harm will come of that, but if you clearly want to do a ceremony for just one of your children, you may have to arrange for the other child to be out at the time. Some ceremonies can be done for each child separately when the other one is not at home.

14. **Q:** I told friends that I was doing ceremonies with my child. Many said that they thought it a strange and unnecessary activity. How should I respond?

   A: Either get new friends or stop telling them what you are doing! Seriously, though, many people do not grasp the idea of ceremonies. Perhaps some examples might help educate them. Remember that many different techniques can be used to help children and their families. Ceremonies are only one of them and may not appeal to everybody.

15. **Q:** Our three children are from another country and we want to incorporate some cultural elements into their ceremonies. How do we get help in doing this?

   A: Libraries and some adoption organizations and associations can help you. Perhaps groups of families can come together and design ceremonies for children who are all from one country or heritage. In Cheri's case, for example, her children were part Native American and they attended an Indian Council where other Native Americans gave them special Native-American names.

16. **Q:** We were doing a ceremony and our cat wandered in and distracted my children. Our cat is nine years old and normally has the run of the apartment. What should we do next time?

   A: Put the cat behind closed doors (perhaps in a bedroom) until the ceremony is over. It will not be for a long time. Just remember to let the cat out after you are finished!

17. **Q:** I have never done anything like this, and I am scared to death to try it. Any advice?

   A: Try to think back to your childhood and your sense of play. Even if you were in a family that discouraged play, most children daydream and fantasize. Maybe you could get down on the floor and do some improvisational playing with your children first. Every situation is different, but picture yourself sitting on the floor and saying that you are from the Tickle Police and were sent to tickle your child. Tickle attacks are fun, especially if they are reciprocal. Children tend to be more spontaneous than adults are. Go to the first ceremony with a sense of eager anticipation and plan to enjoy yourself. You probably will.

18. **Q:** We want to do a ceremony with our son and use puppets, but we really don't have the extra money to spend on them. Do you have any suggestions?

   A: Make simple puppets. Take paper and draw a face with a smile (it does not have to be fancy as long as the smile is clear). Cut out the smiley face and attach it to a popsicle stick or some other blunt stick. Make several puppets in this way, all with different expressions. You and your child can make people and prop puppets (cars, balls, etc.) the same way. Sometimes homemade props can be the best.

19. **Q:** I did a ceremony with my daughter. I worked hard on the ceremony, but instead of making things better, it made things worse. Now what do I do?

   A: You may have hit on a topic your daughter was not ready to deal with or pushed her in ways no one could have predicted. The Chinese have a symbol for crisis that combines danger and opportunity. Rather than see this as a failure, see it as an opportunity. She may need to try therapy, or, if she is in therapy, alert her therapist to what happened. Children sometimes have memories locked inside them of things that either happened before they were able to talk or that they have no words to explain. Issues that have been locked away can be triggered by unpredictable stimuli. Try again. There may be another opportunity waiting around the corner.

20. **Q:** We did a ceremony with our child that really worked, and we'd like to share our experience with you. How do we reach you?

   A: We would love to hear from you about your experiences. We want to continue to learn. Write to us in care of Zeig, Tucker & Co., Inc., 343 Newtown Turnpike, Redding, CT 06896, or e-mail us at ZeigTucker@aol.com.

References

Crowley, Richard J., & Mills, Joyce C. (1989). *Cartoon Magic.* Washington, DC: Magination Press.

Imber-Black, Evan, & Roberts, Janine (1993). *Rituals for Our Time.* New York: Harper Perennial.

Jarrett, Claudia L. Jewett (1982). *Helping Children Cope with Separation and Loss.* Cambridge, MA: Harvard Common Press.

Lifton, Betty Jean (1981). *Lost and Found.* New York: Bantam Books.

Mason, Mary Martin (1995). *Designing Rituals of Adoption for the Religious and Secular Community.* Edena, MN: O. J. Howard Publishing.

Melina, Lois Ruskai, & Roszia, Sharon Kaplan (1993). *The Open Adoption Experience.* New York: Harper Collins.

Pesso, Albert, & Crandell, John (1991). *Moving Psychotherapy: Theory and Application of Pesso System Psychomotor Therapy.* Cambridge, MA: Brookline Books.

Severson, Randolph (1991). *Adoption: Charms and Rituals for Healing.* Dallas TX: House of Tomorrow Productions.

Stein, Chaim (Ed.) (1996). *The Gates of Repentance* (pp. 490–491). New York: Central Conference of American Rabbis.

Viorst, Judith (1971). *The Tenth Good Thing About Barney.* Boston: Atheneum.

Bibliography

The following are books that the authors have found to be particularly useful.

CHILDREN'S BOOKS

Brodzinsky, Anne Braff (1996). *Mulberry Bird: An Adoption Story*. Indianapolis, IN: Perspective Press.

Curtis, Jamie Lee (1996). *Tell Me Again About the Night I Was Born*. New York: Harper Collins Childrens Books.

Freudberg, Judy, & Geiss, Tony (1986). *Susan and Gordon Adopt a Baby*. New York: Random Books Young Readers.

Krementz, Jill (1988). *How It Feels to Be Adopted*. New York: Knopf.

Livingston, Carole (1997). *Why Was I Adopted?* New York: Carole Publishing Group.

McCutcheon, John (1996). *Happy Adoption Day*. New York: Little, Brown.

Viorst, Judith (1971). *The Tenth Good Thing About Barney*. Boston: Atheneum.

Waybill, Marjorie (1974). *Chinese Eyes*. Scottsdale, PA: Herald.

ADULT BOOKS—ADOPTION

Delaney, Richard J., & Kunstal, Frank R. (1993). *Troubled Transplants*. Edmund S. Muskie Institute of Public Affairs, University of Southern Maine, National Child Welfare Resource Center for Management and Administration.

Dorris, Michael (1989). *The Broken Cord*. New York: Harper Perennial.

Jarratt, Claudia Jewett (1982). *Helping Children Cope with Separation and Loss*. Cambridge, MA: Harvard Common Press.

Jewett, Claudia L. (1978). *Adopting the Older Child*. Cambridge, MA: Harvard Common Press.

Keck, Gregory C., & Kupecky, Regina M. (1995). *Adopting the Hurt Child: Hope for Families with Special Needs Kids*. Colorado Springs, CO: Pinon Press.

Melina, Lois Ruskai (1989). *Making Sense of Adoption*. New York: Harper & Row.

Melina, Lois Ruskai (1986). *Raising Adopted Children*. New York: Harper & Row.

Melina, Lois Ruskai, & Roszia, Sharon Kaplan (1993). *The Open Adoption Experience*. New York: Harper Perennial.

Minshew, Deborah H., & Hooper, Christian (1990). *The Adoptive Family as a Healing Resource for the Sexually Abused Child*. Washington, DC: Child Welfare League of America.

Patterson, Eleanora (1987). *Twice Upon-A-Time*. Brattleboro, VT: EP Press.

Sandmaier, Marian (1988). *When Love Is Not Enough*. Washington, DC: Child Welfare League of America.

Watkins, Mary, & Fisher, Susan M. (1995). *Talking with Young Children About Adoption*. New Haven, CT: Yale University Press.

ADULT BOOKS—PARENTING

Barkley, Russell A. (1987). *Defiant Children.* New York: Guilford.

Bennett, Steve, & Bennett, Ruth (1991). *365 TV-Free Activities You Can Do With Your Child.* Holbrook, MA: Bob Adams Inc.

Black, Claudia (1985). *Repeat After Me.* Denver, CO: MAC Publishing.

Blanck, Gertrude (1987). *The Subtle Seductions: How to Be a "Good Enough" Parent.* Northvale, NJ: Jason Aronson.

Borba, Michele, & Borda, Craig (1978). *Self-Esteem: A Classroom Affair.* New York: Harper Collins.

Bozarath-Campbell, Alla (1982). *Life Is Goodbye, Life Is Hello.* Minneapolis, MN: CompCare.

Brokaw, Meredith, & Gilbar, Annie (1987). *The Penny Whistle Party Planner.* New York: Weidenfeld & Nicolson.

Canter, Lee, with Marlene Canter (1988). *Assertive Discipline for Parents.* New York: Harper & Row.

Canter, Lee, & Hausner, Lee (1987). *Homework Without Tears.* New York: Harper & Row.

Clarke, Jean Illsley (1978). *Self-Esteem: A Family Affair.* Minneapolis, MN: Winston Press.

Crowley, Richard J., & Mills, Joyce C. (1989). *Cartoon Magic.* Washington, DC: Magination Press

Dolmetsch, Paul, & Shih, Alexa (1985). *The Kids Book About Single Parent Families by Kids for Everyone.* New York: Doubleday.

Ekman, Paul (1989). *Why Kids Lie.* New York: Penguin Books.

Faber, Adele, & Mazlish, Elaine (1980). *How to Talk So Kids Will Listen and Listen So Kids Will Talk.* New York: Avon.

Farmer, Steven Sandmaier (1989). *Adult Children of Abusive Parents.* New York: Ballantine Books.

Fisher, Gary, & Cummings, Rhoda (1990). *The Survival Guide for Kids with LD (Learning Differences).* Minneapolis, MN: Free Spirit Press.

Fraiberg, Selma H. (1959). *The Magic Years*. New York: Scribner's.

Gesell Institute of Human Development (1985). *Your ____ Year Old Series*. New York: Dell.

Gil, Eliana (1983). *Outgrowing the Pain (A Book For and About Adults Abused as Children)*. New York: Dell.

Hastings, Jill M., & Typpos, Marion J. (1984). *An Elephant in the Living Room: The Children's Book*. Minneapolis, MN: CompCare.

Herman, Judith Lewis (1992). *Trauma and Recovery*. New York: Basic Books.

Herskowitz, Joel (1988). *Is Your Child Depressed?* New York; Pharos Books.

Ingersoll, Barbara (1988). *Your Hyperactive Child*. New York: Doubleday.

James, Beverly (1989). *Treating Traumatized Children: New Insights and Creative Interventions*. New York: Free Press.

Jamison, Kaleel (1984). *The Nibble Theory and the Kernel of Power*. New York: Paulist Press.

Kurcinka, Mary Sheedy (1991). *Raising Your Spirited Child*. New York: Harper Perennial.

Laser, Michael, & Goldner, Ken (1987). *Children's Rules for Parents ("Don't make me put on a sweater when you're cold")*. New York: Harper & Row.

Lemer, Harriet Goldhor (1985). *The Dance of Anger*. New York: Harper & Row.

Madow, Leo (1972). *Anger*. New York: Scribner's.

Morris, Monica (1988). *Last-Chance Children (Growing Up with Older Parents)*. New York: Columbia University Press.

Purdy, Jane A. (1989). *He Will Never Remember: Caring for the Victims of Child Abuse*. Marietta, CA: Cherokee Press.

Ratner, Marilyn, & Chamlin, Susan (1987). *Straight Talk (Sexuality Education for Parents and Kids 4 to 7)*. New York: Penguin Books.

Silverstein, Olga, & Rashbaum, Beth (1994). *The Courage to Raise Good Men*. New York: Penguin Books.

Turecki, Stanley (1989). *The Difficult Child*. New York: Bantam Books.

Welch, Martha G. (1988). *Holding Time (Children with Attachment Disorders)*. New York: Simon & Schuster.

Weisberg, Lynne W., & Greenberg, Rosalie (1991). *When Acting Out Isn't Acting*. New York: Bantam Books.

Index